ANIMAL
WHISPERER

Wild Conversations

By

Suzan Vaughn

FOREWORD

by

Penelope Smith
Animal Communication Pioneer

Cover photo by Stephanie Laird
https://fineartamerica.com/profiles/stephanie-laird

Back cover photo of Suzan Vaughn by Patricia Henry

ISBN -13: 978-0 9814772-4-4

ISBN-10: 0-9814772-4-0

Published by
Medium Masters Publishing
San Luis Obispo, CA 93401

www.suzanvaughn.com
www.animalwhisperer.net

DEDICATION

Here's to the courageous ones. The ones who heard the voice of the Divine and followed a higher calling. The ones who threw off the weighty shackles of approval for the magic of what works to serve their fellow beings on this physical path. The ones who circumvent the disapproval of those whose views don't yet include the future. The ones who heal, listen, inspire, and comfort. The people who slog through the tears and trials of their own personal healing work so they may be a clearer channel that good flows through. This is for the souls who imagine things that precede the limited perceptions of science, because when the effectiveness of the practice becomes undeniable, science seeks to prove it with its accepted protocols. This is for those of us who change things by standing defiantly on the cutting edge of ancient teachings offered for our necessary healing, teachings that seem new and miraculous but were really with us all the time. These words are for the people who are just crazy enough to think they can change the world because, by their visionary actions, they're the ones who do.

DISCLAIMER

To safeguard their privacy, the names of my clients and their animal friends have often been changed. In a few instances, two stories have merged into one.

FOREWORD
BY
PENELOPE SMITH
ANIMAL COMMUNICATION PIONEER

Animal Communicators often have fascinating stories of how they began their profession. Their path may wind through other careers until they discover and study animal communication. Many people work part-time as animal communicators, honing their skills as they deliver their service. Suzan followed this path until she felt moved to focus the talents she had cultivated in her education and careers in psychology, counseling, and journalism into doing full-time work in animal communication.

I remember Suzan as a diligent student of animal communication, demonstrating her bright interest, perception, sincerity, and passion for absorbing what the field of animal communication was all about. These fine qualities now flavor her professional life, highlighted in her warm devotion to helping people with their animal friends.

Suzan's entertaining and fascinating detailed stories of her adventures communicating with animals and their people will captivate you. In these stories, she also includes techniques that have worked for her to connect deeply with animals, her questions and suggestions for animal clients that helped resolve problems, positive results, and some of the limitations and challenges of consultations.

Her book is an enlightening opening to the field of animal communication for the unfamiliar and grist for the mill for eager students.

— Penelope Smith, founding pioneer animal communicator, author of *Animal Talk, When Animals Speak,* and *Animals in Spirit* https://animaltalk.net/

June 2022

PREFACE:
My Telepathic Path Unfolds

When I was growing up, Mr. Ed the Talking Horse, on the television show of the same name, was the only animal I knew that could talk, and even as a 5- or 6-year-old youngster, I knew the horse wasn't really talking. Actor Alan Young, who played Mr. Ed's owner, said the animal trainer started by putting a piece of nylon thread in Mr. Ed's mouth. "But Ed actually learned to move his lips on cue when the trainer touched his hoof. In fact, he soon learned to do it when I stopped talking during a scene! Ed was very smart," said Young.

I loved Mr. Ed. Who knew that 30 years later, I would be sharing my stories of what the animals have said directly to me, including horses like Mr. Ed! No stage, no lights, no voice-overs; just me receiving the information they send and translating it to their people. My intent is to create greater harmony and understanding between the animals and their beloved caretakers.

The surprising and magical nature of animal communication, along with my connection to the realms of higher thought, move the stories from experience to the page, and I hope someday will shift more of these stories to film, not as a comedy, but as a documentary about this phenomenon that helps and heals.

Amid my daily schedule of consultations, a story jumps out, flagging me down to tell it, pressing into my memory because it's unusual or so very usual. Some issues people bring to me are wildly unique, like the tiny terrier who told me he walked down the middle of the street unaware of the danger because, in a recent past life, he had been a large Brahma bull in India where cars and people went around him. Others are very familiar, but never exactly the same, like stories of a rift between fighting animals in a household; or the quiet depth and wisdom of a reptile like Mo, the desert tortoise whose profound inter-dimensional feeling can hardly be translated into words.

Every situation, every animal, and every human is unique. So, I never assume a Golden Retriever enjoys the water (some don't) or that all cats hate water. Inevitably, I'll soon meet a cat client who loves to shower with his person (a true cat story). The skill is to listen with my heart to each unique story. And that's what fills this book: experiences I've had in doing this work and the particular fears and joys of each animal and human unfolding through visions and sentient cues I capture and report.

I didn't know that animals could communicate telepathically until 2001. At around 40 years old, I had been doing psychic readings for people on the weekends for a decade-plus. I was a natural counselor, and when I asked Heaven to send me more inspiring work, people came to me with questions about their animals. My earliest experiences were recounted in my first book, *Dispatches from the Ark: Pages from a Pet Psychic's Notebook*, and are full of reverence and fascination.

Even though I didn't know about animal communication, I did know there was a whole spirit world out there, and in my Baptist upbringing, they called it the Holy Spirit. I believe in such an entity as a helper, an inspirational guide, a teacher, and a communicator that comes from a place of higher consciousness you might call Heaven. Most religious points of view allow for this kind of thinking, though many stop at believing in the direct communication part. Can our souls communicate? This level of discourse comes both from the embodied and the dead. God/Goddess is not inaccessible.

Over the past two decades of specializing in animal communication, I've seen phenomenal growth in this field. From a few practitioners in the 1970s to hundreds of people making a living doing what I do, the profession has enjoyed a growth spurt since I came on board. Some of the evidence of this growth is in Penelope Smith's Animal Communicator Directory, which started with half a dozen listings and at times has had near 200. Penelope is a pioneer in the field and has taught thousands of us how to do this work effectively. As a result of her teachings, there are hundreds more practitioners all over the world.

An old way of communicating, telepathy, is surfacing again today. We once consciously spoke to each other in mind pictures; we are now remembering and recreating what we've lost. The practice of telepathy is in the literature of the ancient Hindus, Egyptians, Greeks, and others. Our minds are cracking open to new dimensions as our old ways of thinking cease to be expansive enough for us here in the West. Other peoples worldwide are ahead of us in the practice of communicating without spoken words.

For Athabaskan Indians in interior Alaska, successful moose hunters must have years of knowledge of the animal. Still, equally important is showing proper respect for the species, the animal's spirit, and the animal's habitat. If the hunter fails in this duty, they say the animals will make the hunt difficult and not offer themselves for food. A ritual of thanksgiving is mandatory whenever an animal presents itself as food. Respect plays a significant part in my own practice. That's one of the first sentiments I send to the animals who open their lives to me.

In the daily routine practice of telepathy, there are many instances of Aboriginal Australians who use the skill to communicate over vast distances. Traditional healers find their way telepathically to the sick, and family members find their way to loved ones in need over vast distances without mechanical communication devices. Telepathy is the only reasonable explanation in thousands of instances.

The Matsés people of Brazil do not delineate between the physical and the spiritual worlds. They believe animal spirits guide hunters to success or failure. If a hunter fails to follow proper respect protocols, they believe the hunt will be fruitless. Abiding by a detailed list of specific taboos for different species, they are careful not to offend animal spirits.

The wordless cries of nature tickle our ears now. The wild and the planet are also calling. More direct communication opens to us, and the animals are asked from a Higher Source to cooperate with our fledgling abilities to get their messages across. I am called and have answered, which I'm sharing here, in gratitude and mystical mindfulness.

INTRODUCTION:
Is This Stuff for Real?

These extraordinary stories would not sit still, demanding like a restless spirit to be born into form. The animals wanted to have their point of view told. So did I. I offer their perspectives because they are so interesting, and I share my own experiences with animals because talking with them seems miraculous.

I admit it was once a stretch for me to consider that animals could use the ancient language of telepathy to communicate directly with us. But after 30 years of witnessing telepathic messaging function in everyday life, I'm here to say it's authentic. I use it with full consciousness and deliberation, but most of us use it unknowingly all the time.

With animal communication, things change and improve for people and their animals. And that's how you can tell it works. For example, the dog no longer darts out the door into the street, the rooster gets off the porch for good, the feral cat offers herself up

for spaying, and the horse no longer shies away from crossties. Behaviors change, and life becomes more peaceful.

Things get better from Tokyo to Tennessee because one of the beautiful things about the new-again yet ancient practice of telepathy is that it defies time and space. So, it can help animals and their people no matter where you and I are in the world. And for some skeptical folks, it's an opportunity to test out the merits of animal communication at a safe distance.

Divine Inspiration or Weird and Scary?

So why do some people think animal communication or intuitive counseling is weird, witchy, or scary? It must be a lack of understanding because this kind of communication happens in everyday life, and there's nothing strange about it. It can save lives.

When you answer the phone, and you already know who's calling; or when you get a sick feeling connected with your child, and you find out she is in an unsafe situation; or maybe when you wake up out of a dead sleep 'knowing' that someone had passed on, telepathy is at work. These hunches and intuitive 'hits' are routine. They're direct messages from Soul Guides looking out for us. Guardian Angels, you might call them.

The practice of animal communication is exacting. For those meticulous practitioners who demand excellence from themselves, continual personal work is a must. That includes self-examination, emotional growth, connection to a Higher Spirit, and the ability to let go of everything and everyone with love.

"Charism" is the term Holy Bible writers use to speak of my calling. In its technical meaning, a charism is a spiritual talent or gift granted by the Almighty for the service of others. (Eph 4.12 and 1 Cor 14.26) Animal communication certainly meets the definition of work that is inspired, connected to service, sometimes prophetic, and always Holy.

This vocation was a gift directly from heaven. And as such, I consider it a sacred trust. The All-In-All presented me with this path by sending me a steady stream of clients as an answer to a pleading prayer. I had asked heaven for more inspiring work, and the animals delivered it.

"The news business is going to kill me if I don't get out," I said to Deity. "Please, show me the way," was my prayer. And within the week, the phone started ringing with requests for animal communication and spiritual guidance from other souls traveling this path. My degrees in psychology and communications had finally merged in a meaningful, vocational way. It was time to expand my new career with first-hand knowledge and practice. My classroom education came from animal communication pioneer Penelope Smith, to whom I will be forever grateful.

In the early days, I tended to my retail website business half the day and offered sessions for my clients the other half of the day. That kept things safe for me. I could tell people who asked about my profession that I was in the eCommerce business, reserving information about animal communication for those who expressed an interest specifically in that.

But there came a time when my wholesalers began to sell their goods directly through Amazon, and my online retail business was no longer viable. I knew that "failure" was purposeful. Spirit required me to ease into animal communication full-time as all my other business ventures fell away. And with 20 years of practice under my belt, I felt ready to declare the gift a true calling.

Amazing Animals

The stories and situations in this book happened to me. The altered names of animals and their people are meant to keep my clients' issues and inquiries confidential. What the animals say or more accurately, show me in pictures is funny, wise, and often unexpected. The tiny African dwarf frog Bandit, for example, asked for a snail friend after his frog companion died. Both the chameleon and the chinchilla conveyed that they didn't like to be touched at all. A dog who tried to sneak food from the dinner table told me he was trying to get some decent human-grade nutrition. And a feral cat client brought her kittens straight to the door of my human client's house after agreeing to get her young cat family sterilized.

The world of the animals is uplifting at times and grievous at other times. I have rejoiced with an animal who finds the perfect forever family, and I have cried for animal clients in the quiet of connection when I "felt" their burdensome lives. I've thanked so many animal helpers who assist me when my communication is fuzzy with doubt. And I've been very grateful after each consult when the animal's messages are crystal clear, lives are better, and people have answers that give them peace.

With great respect and responsibility, it is my sacred lifework to open a channel between people and their beloved animal companions and between people and their soul-level Teachers and Guides. With a profound sense of gratitude and an enormous slice of wonder, I share with you what the animals have told me these past decades.

CONTENTS

SECTION 1

CHATTING WTH A CHEETAH:

WHAT THE ANIMALS TOLD ME

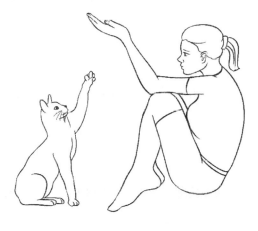

1

Cat-Sitting Jack

Day One

At about 10 a.m. on a warm, sunny Thursday, I stop by my friend Jan's place to visit her cat, Jack. Jan had spontaneously flown to Hawaii for a five-day weekend with a friend, a perk of having retired from airline pilot-dom. Jack offers me a warm welcome.

Jack and I are friends. I've photographed him, slumber partied with him, and brought him tasty treats. Unlike many cats, he likes to be held like a baby, belly-up, but for half a minute at most. After our initial affectionate exchange, Jack lets me know immediately that his top priority is getting outside. Relieved that he's an indoor/outdoor cat, I can oblige him and be his shero.

"Meow, yow, meow," he says while rubbing on the closed cat

door, door frame, and area rug in front of the door. Anything remotely related to the door gets a rubbing.

"Okay. No problem, Jack. Enjoy," I say, lifting the wooden clipboard barrier over the doorless cat door leading to outdoor adventure. Jack perks right up and hops through to the other side.

He jumps up to the wooden railing outside with cat ease and grace; I open the big people's door and step outside it to join him. It's a glorious spring morning with temperatures in the 70s, and on the other side of the railing is a tiny urban jungle made exclusively for Jack. Lush with cool, deep-green ivy, tangled trees, flowering plants and shrubs, and another whole world to explore just up the hill—that's Jack's territory.

Wandering back in and over to the kitchen counter, I spy a note from Jack's human mom, my friend Jan. It contains the phone number of the Hawaii house, so I give her a ring to let her know I'm visiting Jack.

"Hey, girlfriend, how's Hawaii? I stopped by to celebrate finishing the voice-over for the film, but since you're not here, I'm visiting Jack!" I say.

After some small talk, I fearlessly tell Jan that Jack was dying to get outside. I've got the phone with me right now, right on the front steps where Jack is happily rolling around in front of me.

"Oh, don't let him out," says Jan, alarm in her raised voice. "He'll be off and disappear. I've already lost two cats to coyotes in the past few years, and I can't bear to think of losing Jack," she says.

"He's a nocturnal animal, so he comes alive when it gets dark. When you ask him to stay in at night, he's fighting all his instincts to oblige you," I offer.

"I don't care if he *is* nocturnal. He can enjoy the patio," she says. "I can't take the risk. I also want to make it as easy as possible for the upstairs neighbor to watch him. He wants to get out at night when the risk of coyotes is the highest. If he were out, she would worry sick about him until he came back in."

A slight panic creeps up my throat as Jack hops down from the railing and goes under the house out of sight, practically on cue.

"He has a great patio he can enjoy that's safe and allows him to be outdoors," Jan explains. And it's true. This perfectly kitty-appointed outdoor area has everything to make an inexperienced cat happy. But Jack has already stalked bugs in the ivy, chased insects, visited neighboring cats, and climbed trees.

Fear surges. Jack is already out and already out of sight. I soothe Jan's fears and assure her I'll get him in the house as soon as possible. A few more niceties, our conversation ends, and I turn to Jack to begin negotiations.

I make a little pshhhh, pshhhh sound to get his attention should he be nearby.

"Come back, Jack. Come on back in the house now!" I say with trepidation. Jack appears from below and hops up on the elevated walkway. He meows.

5

"Come on in, sweetie. Mom doesn't want you to go out," I tell him aloud.

I need to go out. I love independence. You know all about that, says Jack.

As I come near to scoop him up, he jumps down and sprints away, again out of sight. Negotiations with Jack continue. One of the advantages of telepathic communication is that it doesn't require that the animal is within eye or earshot.

"I do understand about independence. It's on my list of top values. But I'm a little panicked," I tell Jack, sending pictures and feelings to him of my trepidation. Jack does not respond.

Going back into the house, I center myself, link up to Spirit, ask all the animals I've ever helped to assist me now, and open the channel to Jack, wherever he might be. I call his name to get him on the line. I start by sending him respect and understanding for his need to be fancy-free and outside in the natural world.

"Jack, what if you've set up your life path to be eaten by a coyote? Your mom's worst nightmare would come true, and I'd be held partially responsible! I couldn't live with myself." Pleading has already begun.

I communicate with Jack by thinking the words while pictures in my mind play like a movie. These are pictures of what it's like when a predator eats a cat, and the agony his human mom would go through. I follow that image and feeling with a mental picture of his patio, his apartment, and a sense of safety.

I promise that if I have that life path set up, I won't be eaten by coyotes while you are here, he says from his hideaway.

I don't have much room to negotiate. He's gone.

"I want to take that a bit further, Jack, and ask you to consider setting up a long life for yourself with your mom. How about giving her a break from the early kitty deaths she's had to cope with?"

Jack considers. He sends me a picture of looking "forever young." At five or six years old, he's a very young-looking cat.

"Look, Jack, I only want to be here about an hour. So could you come back in an hour?" I'm too worried to hear his answer clearly, but I continue with telepathic negotiations.

You don't trust me, then? He asks.

"I'm at about 60%, but I'm working on getting to 100%. Part of what I don't trust is my ability. I'm having a momentary crisis of competence. If I can't communicate well with you, Jack, that would make me look bad. Plus, what if you decide to say no to my request? I know that's entirely possible, and you could stay out all night. I know the night compels you," I say.

What are you going to do about it? He asks.

"Really, not much I can do. So, I will be waiting for you to be outdoors as much as you need to. I'm asking you to make that about an hour. The bottom line is coming in by nightfall," I say.

Jack considers silently.

Meanwhile, I look at what else I'm supposed to be doing

with this "waiting for Jack" time. I find a bench in the sunshine where I can see the tops of the sand dunes I love. I soak in the scenery, meditate, surround Jack with a cloud of safety, and imagine him coming back into the kitty door safe and sound. Then I go back inside and tend to other computer-related business, waiting. Forty-five minutes pass.

I have come back to 100% trust: in my Higher Source, my animal guides, my helpers and totems, my ability to communicate telepathically, and Jack. I begin a new negotiation with Jack, wherever he is.

"Okay, Jack. I know you and I are in line with Spirit, so why don't you come back when I complete what I'm supposed to accomplish here? How does that sound?" Jack agrees. A pleasant hour passes. Then another ten minutes.

Jack hops in through the kitty door and flops over on his side. I happily thank him, and we dance together.

Day Two

I greet the happy, loving, and affectionate Jack, who is genuinely glad to have company since he has not been sleeping on his mom's neck for a night or two. The joy lasts for about 15 minutes, and then he's jonesin' to get his kitty self outside. But dang. I was hoping to avoid this dilemma again.

Jan's warnings of yesterday fill me with concern. I'm worried that Jack's return was all a bit of luck and concerned about what will happen if Jack is injured or killed while I'm in charge.

Jack is already at the door, meowing.

I start with the "it's not that I don't trust you" dialogue as Jack again rubs on every possible item that could remotely be related to going outside. Picture the scene: on the door, near the door, on the floor at the door, and on the clipboard covering the hole leading to the outdoors. Anyway, I try to distract him.

"Your mom is right, Jack. This patio is a fantastic place that keeps you safe and where you can see everything below. It's like a giant kitty condo up here on the second level. You even have your couch, tree, and natural scratching posts." Jack has followed me outside to the patio where I'm gesturing like Carol Merrill on Let's Make a Deal, showing him the many benefits of his balcony. I've convinced myself how great the balcony is as I take a seat to enjoy the scenery and the patio.

How about for just half an hour out front? says Jack.

"It's not that I don't trust you," I say for the twelfth time. Jack rubs on the door, meowing.

It is that you don't trust me, he counters. I look at that.

"It's because I know you have a right to be and do what you will be and do. I understand your need to be out and about. I relate completely. Can you make it half an hour?" I ask him. I'm into negotiations. Dang it.

Jack rolls on the rug and the door frame.

I reinforce the feelings and pictures related to his safety, visualizing him coming back in half an hour.

"I know you deserve to be trusted, Jack. You demonstrated that yesterday. I'm still working on that today, I guess," I tell

9

him. I stop for a minute and take a breath, remembering first to send Jack respect.

Do you want to make the same deal we made yesterday? Namely, I'll come back when your Higher Sources say you are finished here? he asks me. I waffle, knowing surrendering to my Higher Sources is the right deal to make.

"Uh, let's stick to the half-hour timeline today," I say.

I remove the make-shift clipboard door and Jack is gone in a flash.

I pace a little, worry, and distract myself with plant care while waiting for him. As I settle in and surrender, I catch myself enjoying some quality alone time.

"Jack may need an hour," I keep hearing, which I try to ignore, but it keeps coming back. I try to insist on half an hour but to no avail. One hour later, Jack hops back through the kitty door.

Day Three

I have embraced the idea that cat-sitting Jack is a heavenly gift of solitude and productivity. I've found that I can do work that requires quiet time alone whenever I visit Jack. And it's a mutually beneficial relationship as Jack has an opportunity to go outside.

But this is day three, and I'm on a less flexible schedule. I don't have much time for Jack to be outside, so I consider a leash. I introduce him to a long shoelace that I'm improvising with and it's obvious he's unfamiliar with being tethered to a string. We play with it for a while, and he starts to get the idea as I send him the feeling of being safely tied to a human in that way.

Jack is still tethered to the long shoestring when I pick him up, venture out front and place him on the chest-high railing. I take him to three fun places to visit outside, eventually setting him on a log outside the front door. But he's tired of the leash game and jumps down from the log, which completely snaps his breakaway collar off. I'm left standing there holding a dangling string, the collar, and the ID tag as Jack springs away.

A twinge of fear surges through my psyche, followed by a thought that I'll be waiting for him much longer than I've planned.

"I need you to come back in now," I say.

I make a cup of tea and open the lines of communication to Jack again.

I like not having the bell around my neck, he says. *As you know, I am all about stealth, and I like being silent.*

"Yes, it is one of your greatest talents," I acknowledge.

Like my human mom, I have a tremendous need for independence, he says.

I hear him and can relate.

"I trust Jack will come back soon, whole and happy," I say to Spirit.

Then I focus on getting some writing done, and the time passes rather quickly.

It's about two hours later when Jack hops through the kitty door silently and goes into the kitchen to have a snack. His timing is excellent as I'm finishing up the writing project I brought with me. So, I replace the clipboard/kitty door to keep him in. Jack appears in the living room and rolls around at the front entrance, where the kitty door is now blocked. Then he proceeds to his elevated balcony habitat outside on the deck, drinks rainwater from a giant vase, visits his box, and comes back into the living room.

Holding out the collar with the bell, I ask him to allow me to put it back on. I explain his mom likes the bell because it protects the tiny birds now being hatched. Jack reluctantly allows me to put it back on.

I'm finishing up my work and thinking about packing up, which prompts Jack to rub on the front door. I let him know I'll be in touch telepathically and that his mom will be back in two days.

He purrs and we play until it's time to say goodbye again.

Day Four

Ever in a hurry, I impress that on Jack as I arrive, along with a firm request for him to come back in one hour, no later. Jack and jumps out the kitty door. I take the meow to mean *whatever*. I can see I will not be in control of this situation.

I'm grateful for Jan's condo and making the most of my time in this secluded writing studio with a view, while Jack gallivants who knows where, through the flora and fauna of the neighborhood. It's replete with hundreds of made-for-kitty hiding places of ivy beds and overgrown vegetation.

I have plans for the day, but the truth is those plans are flexible. I reflect on that as time passes, opening myself to what my Higher Sources want me to do today. It looks like the message is "get some writing done."

Jack, looking worn out and panting a bit, jumps through his kitty door four hours later.

"Dang, Jack," I say to him as he rolls around on the carpet, "we're certainly on different time schedules. I guess we're going with the flow today...."

Hmmm. My Higher Sources know my schedule is flexible today, and their plan for me is writing and solitude. I also realize I've been saying I need more time alone. Here it's being offered to me, and I'm almost missing it by resisting it!

Day Five

Fishy, smelly, wet canned cat food is on Jack's mind today, above going outside, which is a surprise. But in a rare move, I deny him, feeling he'll be more motivated to come back in if he's got a food incentive. I tell him it'll be available when he returns, but he needs to go out first.

One-shoulder hug, and he's off into the wild blue yonder where his collar is now. The breakaway collar has broken away somewhere where I'm not supposed to be letting him go.

"Could you bring the collar back, Jack?" I ask him.

I love being bell-less. Besides, you don't believe I will bring it back. Dogs are for fetching, he says.

"Ya got me there. But I do believe our Higher Sources could put it in my path where I could see it and pick it up. Would you be willing to wear it again?" I ask.

Not right now. Maybe for my mom, he says.

Once Jack is outside and out of sight, I choose the most nutritious brand from the six remaining cans of cat food, put some of it in his bowl, and go on about my business.

Fumbling around with computer and power cords and providing customer service at the same time, I'm caught off guard when Jack hops back in an hour later, eats the food, and is quickly gone again. So much for my lame idea to lure him in with food and close the cat door.

Although Jack has followed what I said would happen, namely that he needs to go outside before eating, it's not exactly how I envisioned it. The food lure was an epic failure. I tried it to leave closer to the time I had planned. But he had other ideas and followed the literal instruction I gave him (as animals do) to go outside first, then eat. I didn't plan on the part where he went back out again after eating.

I check my anxiety level. Today, I have set appointments — trust level: 80%.

Jack's schedule, as always, works out. He returns after two and a half hours and I'm right on time with the rest of my day.

Offering Jack love, safety, and affection as I turn the key to lock him back inside again, I see a happy reunion with his human mom the next day. Jack hops up into the window to watch me leave.

I thank him for being my cat companion and teacher for the week.

2

Mutiny and Miracles

It was a four-cat mutiny at the home of Meredith and John, led by Nugget, a sassy, long-haired orange cat with tufts of fur on his ears, making him look a little like an orange lynx. Nugget was staging a hunger strike, and the entire clowder (a group of cats) had stopped eating. The human couple called me to get to the bottom of the problem. They had just purchased a whole case of a particular cat food they thought all their cats liked.

"We've been trying different wet food brands and flavors, but we continue to struggle to find food that provides proper nutrients and that they will eat. They are playing as usual and seem healthy overall except for this loss in appetite," Meredith reported.

Nugget paced in the background as I spoke to Meredith on the phone. He felt restless. This full-of-adventure orange Creamsicle© cat was coming into a lot of mischievous energy, and he was ready to unleash it onto the natural world outside. His people had plans for him to be an indoor cat, and I had to find a diplomatic way of letting them know this wasn't going to happen.

"In addition to losing interest in food, Nugget often meows at us and seems to be trying to tell us something. He frequently jumps over to the neighbor's balcony, which causes us anxiety," they said.

Nugget was a charmer in his picture and tuning into his youthful energy was fun. He told me he was indeed an adventure-seeker. He was sorry his people were stressed out when he finally made his way to the neighbor's balcony and the great outdoors. But he said he had to go. He was anxious to let his people know that he had to interact directly with nature to fulfill his life as a happy cat.

"I guess we're going to have to stop ignoring his requests to get outside," Meredith said.

Nugget longed to hunt, roll in the dirt and grass, climb a tree, and feel his heightened senses during the night. Even as a neutered adolescent male feline, his nocturnal self was emerging with gusto.

Cat number 2 in this household, Hank, hung his head low over his food bowl when I asked him what he thought of their diet. And in the telepathic picture he sent me, he wasn't eating, just staring at the food.

Hank had a lot of trouble with the current cat diet. The canned food was just okay nutritionally, but the dry food was without much nutritional benefit, and his body felt it. He showed me that his kitty butt was draggin'.

As a group, the cats were thrilled that their considerate people were calling to ask me about their diet. There was a group feeling of relief and satisfaction they sent me to convey that. I also offered their people several inexpensive ways to increase the nutritional value of the cat food they already had in the garage.

With tools and homework for resolving the food issue, Meredith moved on to her next concern.

The Litter Box

"I wanted to mention I've noticed a strong ammonia smell in their favorite litter box, and I'm wondering if anyone has a UTI," she said. "Also, we treated three of them for fleas with (a popular liquid application) about a week ago and plan on administering a tablet to treat tapeworms once we confirm the fleas are gone."

Posey, a 7-year-old white-chested female calico, wanted to weigh in on this.

The strong smell is our bodies trying to flush out the toxic anti-flea chemicals, Posey said. I explained how keeping fleas out of the house was a top priority, adding that we wanted them to be healthy and comfortable, too.

Posey was in significant discomfort, experiencing hair loss, scabs from scratching, and reactions from the flea tablet. The calico let us know that all the cats needed to have a few weeks on an immune-strengthening diet before they could handle the administration of another heavy-duty chemical. But they all fully understood why we put these chemicals on

17

them after I explained it.

Meredith said, "Posey will not let me put (the drops) on her, so I give her tablets once in a while. I would love your insight on her skin problems and how I should treat her for fleas."

As I scanned Posey's body, I saw only an occasional flea. I asked Meredith to consider reacting when she saw a flea instead of taking the road of preventing the fleas, particularly with this sensitive-skinned cat. Meredith and John were willing to wait for the cats to get stronger and reduce doses appropriately. (I recommend a natural flea remedy from Green Hope Farms Animal Wellness Collection at https://www.greenhopeessences.com/ animal-wellness)

Meredith, John, and their cat family have been wonderful clients of mine over the years, and together we've experienced some inspiring effects of animal communication. These two are the couple that told our story in one of my YouTube movies about animal communication that, for me, was uber fulfilling.

The movie details the story of Isabelly, a young, feral Siamese cat who had kittens near their home in the California desert. After our session, this feral animal agreed to fully cooperate with humans in the sterilization process. Isabelly's story seems miraculous and points directly to the effectiveness of animal communication.

Isabelly lived in some bushes in their woodsy apartment complex. No human *owned* her, but John and Meredith fed her on their upstairs apartment landing to help her out.

"She was an outdoor cat. She would allow us to pet her, but

18

she had no interest in coming inside. Then she showed up pregnant one day, and we didn't know how to help her since she was definitely a stray. Soon after that, we saw her with two kittens.

"We had used Suzan's services before on health and behavioral issues for our other cats, so we decided to talk to her about this," said Meredith.

It was up to me to determine if Isabelly would consent to being fixed and having her kittens sterilized too. I explained to Isabelly that humans asked cats to undergo the sterilization process to ensure all cats were healthy and happy. And Isabelly asked me to show her the details of what I was asking her to submit to.

Explaining the process of sterilization to the cat was an intricate transmission of images but necessary for her to understand everything we were asking of her. First, she would go from the wide-open spaces of the outdoors to being confined in a carrier; then, she would be fasting in a bedroom. Next, she would be transported by car, examined by veterinarians, put under general sedation, and opened up for major surgery. She would return to consciousness in a small cage in an unfamiliar place, go back into a car for transport back home, and recover in John and Meredith's guest room for a two-week rehabilitation period. After that, the couple would allow Izzy and her kitties to decide if they wanted to go back to the wild or become domestic.

This little mama cat said yes to participating, which warmed my heart, but it also surprised me, even though I'd had that same success with feral cats. I crossed my fingers and hoped

I had received her message clearly.

Meredith trusted the process and made the appointment to get the cats spayed as soon as the kittens were old enough to be on their own. She made only one appointment for Isabelly, but this mama cat had plans of her own. The day before the appointment, the vet's office called to say there had been a cancellation and asked Meredith if she wanted to take the other two slots for the kittens. She said yes, steadfast in her trust in the communication.

"I was stressed because I thought, okay, I have these appointments, but I have no idea how I will catch the kittens and take them to the vet. I was pretty sure I could get Isabelly because she let me pet her, but I had no idea how I would get the kittens in there.

"The night before the surgery, I heard her meowing at the front door. This was kind of unlike her. She usually sat quietly and waited for me to appear on the porch. So, I opened the front door and, lo and behold, there was a kitten right on the doorstep.

"I was able to grab the one kitten and put her in the room, and then about 20 minutes later, I heard the same meow, and there was a second kitten right at my doorstep. Animal communication made all the difference in helping these intelligent cats understand what we were trying to do. Once they understood, they willingly participated, and she brought her kittens to me. It was a fantastic experience," Meredith told me.

"The kittens were living under a bush, so Isabelly had to convince them to go up the steps and come to our doorstep where there's a lot of noise, and there aren't a lot of places to hide. It took a giant leap of faith for Isabelly to present her kittens to me.

"It would have been tragic to shove her into a carrier and take her to get sterilized while she was terrorized and not knowing what would happen. It would have been terrible to have that be her only encounter with people," Meredith said.

I agree. This soul-to-soul agreement became a physical expression of cooperation and trust between felines and humans. I'm so grateful to have played my part; it still makes me smile.

3

Telly Hails a Nurse

Relief swept over Cassie as the front tires of her car pulled into the driveway. It had been a long, exhausting, and emotional day at work. An RN on the COVID-19 ward at the local hospital, Cassie fought back tears as she arrived home. She thought she saw a flash of reflection in the headlights through watery eyes: Was it wild eyes in the bushes? Cassie wasn't sure. Or maybe, she considered, looking through tears distorted her vision. She blinked three times to bring the image into focus, and her eyes finally saw the outline of a cat.

The big tabby was reluctant to move much. He hissed instead, insisting that everyone and everything keep their distance from his aching body. He was hurting. His tail was broken, and putting weight on his left back leg sent a screaming pain up from the paw pad. One of the cat's ears looked chewed up, and his cheek was twice the size it should have been. He was in such bad shape that it was impossible to tell his age, especially from a distance like this.

Both curiosity and caretaking collided in Cassie as she approached the bushes. She spoke gently to what she had finally discovered: a tabby cat in her hedge. "It's OK, kitty. I'm here to help you," she said. The cat hissed and backed up, threatening to run. Cassie backed up too.

Too tired to have any fight left in her, Cassie went inside, grabbed a can of tuna out of the cupboard, dumped it on a saucer for the cat, and wondered if he'd still be there when she took it outside. He was still there, just harder to see, and he made no move toward the food.

"That's what I can do for you now, kitty," she told him as she headed for a smidgen of self-care. She had put a luxurious bubble bath on her calendar and kept that appointment in keen focus. The bath that cleanses; the bath that renews. The bath that she'd found herself asleep in more than a few times lately, resulting in dragging herself out of the inevitably cold water and into bed for a few hours before life-and-death duty called again and again.

Cassie set up a session with me to relay the message to the tabby that she was there to help. By the time I met him, the cat had backed way up into a beautifully landscaped hedge, trying to stay hidden to heal or die. When I contacted him, he said he needed a bit more time but would allow the help. I showed him everything we planned to do with and for him, including the carrier, the trip to the busy office with anxious animals in it, the vet exam, the feeling of a car ride, and the touching and probing of the body during the examination.

"This is how we care for you," I told him. And he said he'd go along with the plan very soon.

I always triple-check when hurt or feral cats say yes to veterinary care, so I went through my routine of double-checking and got the same answer. Cassie carried on with her life, honoring the cat's request to give him more time.

The workday brought Cassie a day of COVID deaths and emotional hammers, so she looked forward to the distraction of whether she would see the cat in the hedge when she got home. And for a week, she did. His reluctant trust grew as she talked to him, but if she made a move toward him, he took his leave quickly.

In the second week, she tried my direction to touch him with a branch she held in her hand or to stroke him with a small but long stick while he ate. After another week, she was able to touch him very lightly.

She called him Telly, after Telly Savalas, the actor who played Lt. Theo Kojak in the television series *Kojak*. Savalas' character was a tough detective in the late 1980s and early 1990s, known for his no-nonsense ways and his ever-present lollipop. I kept in touch with Telly, letting him know Cassie intended to help.

It didn't take much longer before Cassie gained the feral cat's trust, found the moment to slide him into a carrier, and took him to the veterinarian to assess his wounds; a much easier process than she'd imagined.

Telly returned from the veterinarian with his head spinning and his body dragging. But he knew help had arrived in the nick of time. I spoke to him about relaxing into the healing inside the house, letting him know Cassie had agreed to nurse him back to health. He released a psychic sigh of relief and had no great urge to get back outside.

Fit as a fiddle is the image he showed me a few months later. That's when Cassie called me after the healed young cat sprinted out of the front door in a flash. Frantically, she called him back, but he kept going toward the stand of trees about 500 yards in the distance.

He sent me the feeling that he had to go. He had to recover from the medications for a while, and he had to get out into nature to do it.

Cassie was a basket case. She continuously visualized scenarios in which coyotes attacked Telly. She considered restricting his outdoor exposure, making him an indoor cat.

He was gone 19 days, and then he came back.

There is no way I will be an indoor cat, he told me. *I love nature, and I feel better outside. I understand how to be in that environment but not so much inside this structure. Where are the birds? Where are the trees?* he asked. Telly was poised to spring out the door ASAP, and Cassie signed up for a session with me in hopes of implementing a new negotiation.

"I'd like to talk with Telly about going outside," she said. "I've tried everything: all kinds of interactive toys, two cat trees. But he's becoming frustrated with me and wants to go outside." No kidding, I thought silently.

"I've been researching cat-proof fencing attachments and catios (cat patios). I'm terrified of letting him go back outside after his nineteen-day absence and the condition I found him in. So, I need to figure out if he'd be OK with a catio enclosure. Or I could adjust the fence height, and he'd be only in the backyard. Or, if I let him go back outside like he used to, he would have to agree to go out only during the day and be back by dinnertime," she said, breathless after listing all the options on offer.

"The coyotes are howling at night lately. And cars drive so fast down my road. Lots of worries on my end," she added. Meanwhile, Telly had no such concerns, saying he was a very capable cat, although he was ever so grateful for her help.

My discussions with Telly told me he was interested in becoming her domestic cat companion. Still, he had no idea that, once his body healed, there would be concern about letting him back outside in nature where he felt he belonged. He enjoyed Cassie's attention and support but could not be content without spending a considerable portion of his life out in the elements.

Telly understood and noted Cassie's concern for him. He showed me he was a savvy outdoor cat and knew just what to do when the scent of a coyote was in the air. He reminded Cassie that his destiny was something he had chosen before incarnating into a cat body. He relayed to me that he didn't think he'd chosen to be taken by a predator this time around.

I solidified the option Cassie offered and asked what he would prefer. A catio; a higher fence, and backyard; or an agreement to be home by dinnertime and the freedom to wander close-by. He agreed to option three.

Months later, he was still keeping his agreement with Cassie to return home by dinnertime. She felt good about the arrangement.

Animal communication has been very successful in making deals with cats who have no intention of giving up nature during their lifetimes. But when folks ignore the need they know is there, some cats disappear as soon as they can get out, and they never come back. Some re-home themselves into places where they have the option of going outside, or they become members of a feral cat colony.

Negotiating a curfew has been super successful. I've made the deal to come in at dark with many cats and have had fantastic success even though cats are nocturnal and come into heightened awareness when the sun goes down. So, it's a big ask.

Animals who come into our lives are eager to be good domestic partners, but they call on us to respect and honor what they need to lead a fulfilling life. When I look at a higher level of consciousness, they show me that humans are learning to let go and understand that they do not control their animals' life paths and deaths.

4

Birthday Cat

Frances woke up feeling melancholy, and she wasn't sure why. She slogged through morning coffee, did her best to get through a slow day at work, and finally found herself on the way home, exhausted and restless.

The autumn leaves had just turned to brilliant fall colors on this rainy October evening, and Frances' commute was congested. Cars, strung out in long lines, meandered home an inch at a time through rush hour on the Murfreesboro, Tennessee freeway. Frances was talking on the phone when a small light-colored object caught her eye just in front of the passenger side front tire.

"I screamed into the phone, threw it on the passenger seat,

31

and jumped out of the car, stopping traffic in both directions," she told me. "I couldn't believe what the object was: a tiny kitten. I didn't know if the kitten would spook and run, but she didn't. She was dirty and scared but unharmed. However, she wasn't used to riding in the car and was already terrified, so she cried continuously during the 30-minute drive home.

"I was definitely not in the market for another animal, but I also believed that our paths hadn't crossed by accident," she said. She named the little tabby Sadie.

"That's when I remembered it was my deceased dad's birthday," she said, "and I wished him a happy day, wherever he was. Memories flooded my mind about his 47th birthday when I was nine years old," she said. "He'd said 'no' just a few months earlier to me getting a kitten, so I decided I would give him one for his birthday. You can't give away a birthday present, right?" Frances laughed, explaining her young logic. She wondered about that connection now, on his special day, when he'd accepted the gift and kept the kitten years earlier.

Meanwhile, the restless orange kitten in the front seat was a wild cat, a scrapper, which muddied the waters about six months later as I tried to find out why she was peeing and pooing all over the house. I assumed that up to now, she had eliminated anywhere she wanted to, so I asked her. And, as usual, the issue was not what my intellectual mind thought.

"Do you understand what the cat box is for?" I asked.

Yes, she answered.

"Is there any reason you would not want to go there?" Always my standard follow-up question.

Yes, she said, showing me a dog in the household who was overly interested in following her through the house and observing her litter box habits in an up-close-and-personal kind of way. And there was more.

Sadie's body attracted my attention. A body scan revealed something moving in the gut, which is usually my sign for parasites. In addition, I began to get the sensation of a urinary tract infection. Dang. Multiple physical issues.

I reported my findings to Frances, who said she'd seen blood in the cat's urine. Still, after two rounds of antibiotics and no change in Sadie's problems, Frances returned to the vet to discover parasites were multiplying at an alarming rate in Sadie's gut. That confirmed the picture I had seen.

I wasn't happy about the parasites or the UTI, but I was feeling good about the accuracy of the reading. As a former career journalist, accuracy is one of my fundamental values when it comes to animal communication sessions. I'd been doing interviews my whole career, and this wasn't much different except for how the information arrived. Not on a word train, but a picture, a sense, a flash, or a sound transmission offering itself to me to translate into words. My most often used medium is visual, so these images of what was going on in Sadie's body played like a movie in my head.

Frances had many other concerns, complaints, and questions for this six-month-old kitten. I went through the list, letting her know what was expected of a cat in this domestic situation.

"I understand she likes to play rough, but biting and scratching me or the furniture, especially my wicker chest, is not okay. She has plenty of scratching posts," Frances told me, and I translated.

"It's okay for her to play in the tub, but not with my toilet paper." I passed this along.

"I also need her to understand that she must not pee or poop anywhere except in her litter boxes." Again, I translated.

"I need her to trust me when I put her in the car, in her carrier. She must understand that one day in the future, I will take her on a very, very long plane ride. I will do whatever I must to keep her on board with me and not in cargo, but it will require her to be perfectly quiet. It will be hard for both of us but worth the effort," she said. I translated.

It's always a good idea to make sure an animal who will be flying understands everything they'll be going through, including quarantines, take-offs, and landings. For the animal, being off the ground can be very disorienting. It helps when they have the details about what will be happening during travel.

Sadie agreed to work on these issues and did incredibly well during the airplane flight. The two arrived at their destination, a new home a few states away. And Sadie was ready to go outside and explore her pristine wilderness in the back of the place.

Sadie didn't make these critical changes overnight. Like

34

most cats who start as feral or with feral parents, it took Sadie time to understand her domestic role. But animal communication helped to change her instinctual leaning toward a wilder life to finding a compromise in her new domestic situation.

5

Hobbes the Sizable

The sizeable striped cat came through loud and clear during my preliminary greeting before the official session began. He was a formidable personality, this new cat client of mine who was next on my schedule. His countenance was enormous, and as I merged with him spiritually, he felt like a cougar, panther, or another large and imposing cat.

His name was Hobbes, an 18-pound giant of a cat who ruled his small backyard jungle with a strong scent he spread around generously.

As I tuned in, he felt so delighted to be outside: so wildly grateful to be in his element. As I spent a minute "in his skin," a forceful feeling of liberation came through; to once again be able to touch nature; to have and hold territory, and to claim it via marking. Cat bliss!

Hobbes had some characteristics that reminded me of the Egyptian Mau cat. He was strong and on the wild side. I couldn't imagine keeping this nature-loving cat indoors, but that had been his fate for the first 12 years of his life. Things had recently changed when he came to live with Diane.

Hobbes made it clear he would be going outdoors. He craved nature, yearned for trees, dreamed of bugs and rolling in the grass and dirt, and Diane honored his needs.

After three months, Diane reported that Hobbes had settled in nicely but still had some problems with playing too roughly.

"I want to ask him about the biting and scratching. I am very respectful and kind toward him, and I don't understand why he resorts to that behavior all too often and suddenly. Why is he so touchy?" Diane asked.

Hobbes explained that his man liked to play rough in his last household. The man put on heavy gloves to do it. Hobbes also said he had no other place to express himself because even though he protested loudly at the door, he was not allowed to go outside.

I explained to Hobbes that his new person was fragile, and that claws and fangs could do her and her house guests plenty of harm. That led to a chat about affection, how humans feel about it, and how best to offer it.

A few days after our consultation, Diane wrote to me, "In the morning, Hobbes usually jumps up on my bed to greet me and get a little head rub, very briefly. But this morning, he jumped up on my bed for his head rub and settled in with a paw on my shoulder.

He also rested his head on my shoulder and pressed gently against my cheek, purring softly.

"He stayed that way a very long time. It was so sweet.

"I credit Suzan for much of this new trust and affection with Hobbes. It's incredibly helpful to have this level of communication and understanding with my animals, especially when we have all come together as older critters with many varied life experiences.

"She has taught me much, and I am grateful! Thank you, Suzan."

Well, I want to thank YOU, Diane, for believing in and using animal communication to improve your inter-species relationships. You are much appreciated.

6

A Healing Solution

Mavis sometimes worked long hours as a nurse at the local hospital, and she felt guilty about leaving her cat Delta at home. So, she decided to foster two kittens to keep her cat company while she was away. But after a few weeks of hissing and tension, Mavis wondered if she had made a big mistake. Adding to her stress was the pressure to work it out because foster homes were in short supply due to a growing number of cats.

"Even though I love my one-on-one relationship with Delta," she said, "I felt she might want some companionship. I also feel restricted because I feel guilty about leaving her alone for too long. She seems stressed when left alone nowadays."

Mavis loved animals, and fostering Dickery and Doc, a pair of 5-week-old kittens, sounded like a 3-cat win-win-win situation.

Unfortunately, Delta's hissing at the kittens caused Mavis to wonder if the pair were a good fit and if her goal to offer companionship to her cat was the right move. By now, she had become attached to Dickery and Doc and worried they wouldn't be adopted as a pair if she returned them once her foster cycle was over. Mavis wanted them to stay together.

She was also concerned about her original cat companion Delta. As the session began, Mavis wanted to know whether Delta would be all right as an "only cat," how she felt when Mavis was gone to work and whether she would prefer a dog companion instead. Were the kittens offering her companionship as intended?

Delta showed me that she sniffed at the kittens occasionally and, at other times, growled to say *this is my territory*. She wasn't attached to the kittens in the way we humans form attachments, and she understood them as temporary house guests. The information came from their human mom, who was undecided about whether these cats would be fosters or permanent residents. Delta said she was confused about whether the kittens were staying or going.

Are they supposed to be part of my clowder? She asked me. *Because I can easily adjust to life without other cat companions. Mavis is the one who is stressed when I am left alone, not me.*

"Ok," I relayed. "How would you feel about a dog companion?"

She didn't want a dog either. What this wise cat told me she wanted was a little surprising.

I want Mavis to resolve some things that are up in the air in her personal life so she can regain her calm. I also want to focus on a business partnership with her. She's a healer, a massage therapist. I want to be a healing partner to Mavis's clients. That healing job is essential to me, she transmitted.

Mavis was excited about this message. She was grateful that Delta wanted to be a part of her healing team.

"I've been thinking about returning my practice to this home space. I want to move it out of the building it's in, which doesn't feel good anymore. Some new tenants have moved in, making the place feel unsettled. There are arguments in adjoining offices now that didn't use to be a problem. I'm thrilled Delta is reinforcing a decision I've been struggling with for some time now," she said.

Mavis was also relieved that Delta felt fulfilled as a single cat. It turned out that the consultation was partly to allow her to let go of the kittens. She felt overly responsible for giving them a home instead of sticking to what she had agreed to do.

This animal-loving woman had simply agreed to foster the kittens after feeling guilty about her cat being alone. But what she really needed was a reevaluation of complex changes she needed to make in her work life. Delta reminded her she needed to ramp up her own self-care, and the cat gave her a glimpse of a calmer 1-cat future amid overwhelm.

In closing the session, we asked the kittens to help attract their ideal homes while Mavis completed her fostering term. I let all the cats know what the new arrangement was going to be, and everything turned out wonderfully. The foster situation ended in a brilliant adoption in which the kittens went to live in a happy home together.

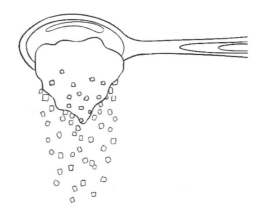

7

Dorado Claims His Place

Mona adored her four cats, and Dorado was her favorite. She said she couldn't live like this anymore and needed help and answers. She said Dorado was "acting out" by peeing all over the house. So I put my Inspector Clouseau hat on, pulled out my psychic magnifying glass, and began the sleuthing game with Dorado, a 6-year-old male.

In meditation, I opened to messages from this wise orange cat as the soft sounds of Native American flutes wafted through my consciousness. The music of the people who have long honored telepathic communication between people and animals took me to a higher place where a soul-level interchange of ideas flows.

"I see that you are peeing throughout the house, Dorado. Are you afraid?" I asked.

Not exactly, he said.

"Is it territorial?"

Yes. I am feeling insecure. I have no territorial security, he said.

I wanted to ensure that no other animals inside the house were to blame, so I double-checked Dorado's relationship with the other three cats in the household, but I saw no trouble there.

"Is it a person or an animal?"

Person. A man, he told me, and I reported it to Mona.

There had been a lot of trouble with a neighbor, she said. He was the type of guy who kept dogs, trained them to be vicious and protective, and looked for opportunities to encourage them to attack any cat that came on his property. He hated cats.

Mona had called the police, who promptly ordered her neighbor to contain the dogs instead of positioning them on the front porch unrestrained. The man also trained his dogs to frighten folks walking near his house by encouraging them to bark and snarl aggressively.

I sent all of these images to Dorado, double-checking that it was this particular neighbor that had him worried.

Yes, he said. *That man has my human mom in a twisted state of stress. She sends many pictures of this neighbor hurting or maiming cats. And there's constant tension and a flow of angry images.*

Mona has asked me to make the danger clear to the cat. Dorado told me he understood my communication about the man and the potential threat he posed.

"Would it help to have your scent around the outside of the house," I asked him, and he said it would.

I instructed Mona to sprinkle a tablespoon of urine-soiled litter in several places around the house's exterior to help Dorado's insecurity issues. He felt better at the clarity gained from the communication and having his smell spread all over his property boosted his confidence.

Part of this consultation included a body check to see if I felt any pain when he urinated or a feeling of any blockage that I could detect, but I didn't see or feel anything.

"Dorado," I asked, "Is this physical?"

No, he told me. *Emotional. Territorial.*

"Ok," I said, "got it."

"Check these findings with your veterinarian," I added, "and if you see or feel that Dorado is not feeling well, you should take him in for a check-up."

My person needs a barrier between this house and the neighbor's energy, he showed me. Mona and I got right on that energetically.

We took a few cleansing breaths. We invited our animal guides and teaching companions from a higher plane to help us. We imagined a block wall between her and the neighbor man's home, attitude, anger, garage, dogs, and anything else we could think of that we needed to block off. We dropped

47

an image of that block wall into physical reality by sensing it, smelling it, and knowing it to be there.

You might call what Mona and I erected an imaginary wall, but it set the intention that she had clear boundaries regarding the neighbor's ill intentions. And it gave Dorado a sense of security. When I chatted with Mona later, she told me the intensity she felt coming from the neighbor's house lessened.

I've often recommended sprinkling the scent of an animal who lives inside out into the yard and garden. A few tablespoons will do. It works great for those inside who are concerned about wild or feral beings that live outside their homes. This technique often works even for cats who don't go outside. They know their scent is out there, declaring that this is *their* territory. It makes them feel much more settled.

After expressing his worries, Dorado confined his peeing to the five litter boxes inside the house. This orange cat was keenly aware of his scent all around the structure's exterior now, delineating his very own territory. His feeling of security grew, and he no longer needed to mark inside the house with urine.

8

British Blues

Pinned helplessly against your airline seat during the inertia of takeoff: that was the first feeling I sent to Mickey and Shelby, a young pair of solid blue-gray British Shorthair kittens less than two months old. But that was only part of what they were about to experience on their journey to their final destination, which was their forever home 300 miles away.

My human client Fran let me know that the kittens would be traveling from their breeder's home in Oregon to her house in California in two days. And that was going to involve cars, carriers, and airplanes. My job as their communicator was to let them know about everything they were likely to encounter on their journey and give them a preview of their new life.

So, I translated the message from Fran to the kittens: "It will be a long day with many noises and smells, but we will try to keep you comfortable. We are delighted to have you come live with us.

"There are three things we would like very much. Please try to learn your names, use the scratching posts and boxes, and be willing to try new food and flavors," Fran said.

Fran also sent me pictures of herself, her husband, and their home, which I transmitted to the kittens. By the time they arrived, they were entirely familiar with the house's layout. We had a great session with these youngsters who were excited, happy to be together, playful, and sweet. And Fran was thrilled once they arrived.

"They were friendly and unafraid and seemed familiar with what we looked like and where each room in the house was located. They must have felt so good about that!" she said.

They surely did. Contented to be fully informed about what was going on made everything super smooth for Mickey and Shelby. And Fran further opened lines of communication with these fabulous felines at home.

The kittens felt older and wiser than their young years even though I was tuned in to their soul-level selves. Fran agreed.

"Through our dialogue with them, I got the sense that they have an awareness beyond their age. The kittens already knew that people kept kittens in a small room at first and asked about that, for example. Mickey knew and asked about going outdoors. That has enabled me to communicate with them about now versus the future, or cat things versus people things.

"I say things to them like, 'When you are bigger, you can do such and such. Please be patient right now since you are too little,' or 'That's not a cat toy, no!' They pause and listen, and I stay patient. They are still impulsive, but I don't feel they're willful or frustrated. We're in a genuine dialogue! Of course, I still watch them, so they don't get hurt, but it feels as though they appreciate the communication. All in all, pretty awesome, I'd say!"

And I'm sure they will all live happily ever after.

COWS

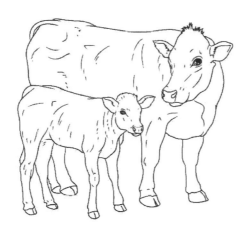

9

Cow 704

Cows and their calves have been part of my practice from the beginning, and 704 was the first one I ever witnessed giving birth. On a perfect spring morning when the green rolling hills of central California were in full flower, Cow number 704 was in the late stages of labor by the time I arrived at the ranch. Long-time clients of mine, Jeff and Joan, invited me to be a part of the birth of their latest addition to the farm.

The birth was difficult and took longer than Jeff felt comfortable with, so he lined up the 4-wheeler to help the little bull exit from the womb into the waiting world. Wrapping chains gently around the calf's chest and head while it was still mostly in utero wasn't easy, but Jeff was strong and managed to get the chain in place.

Joan positioned herself in the seat of the small vehicle and backed up slowly at Jeff's direction. Soon the couple pulled the newborn from his watery sack, and gallons of fluid spilled on the ground along with the calf. The mother rose to her feet and turned to see her calf. She nudged and cleaned him, willing him to stand up, and it wasn't long before he did. His wobbly legs were soon planted more solidly on terra firma, and he gained some stability.

As was his custom, Jeff kissed the little calf on the head to welcome him into the world, which startled the newborn and sent him running.

"The calf shot out, crossed the road, shot past the neighbor's fence, and disappeared," said his wife, Joan.

Cow 704 ran after her new calf at full speed but soon became confused. She then returned to the last place she had nursed her newborn calf, which, according to Jeff, is the natural way a cow in his herd would react to a missing calf.

"Cattle are drawn to the last place they nursed their calf. So, if the calf gets lost, they don't go to where they last saw the calf. They go to where they last nursed the calf. That's where the challenge came in, and we looked for the calf at the neighbor's ranch for about five hours," said Jeff.

He said that generally, if they had taken the cow over the fence to the neighbor's ranch and let her go, she would have focused back on their property toward the area where she had last nursed her newborn. And that's why they called me.

"Suzan talked to 704, and her idea was to load up the cow and take her over there to the neighbor's place to look for the calf," said Joan.

"What Suzan helped us with was two big things. Getting a cow out by herself, then into the corral, and finally into a trailer is a big ordeal. But after Suzan talked to 704, I walked behind her, Joan opened the gate, and the cow literally walked right across the barnyard, across the corral, turned around, and walked into the trailer with no prompting from us," said Jeff.

Joan chimed in, "Which was amazing because she's not one of the friendlier cows we've trained for the fair or anything. She's had no human interaction other than feeding and was very calm about it. She just walked in, and it was like she was saying, '*Okay, let's go.*' We took her across the street and let her out. She started sniffing around, looking under bushes; she was looking for her calf. It blew both of us away."

"We were both astounded because that was not characteristic bovine behavior," Jeff added. "Normally, she would have looked around and then run back to the fence headed toward home, but she looked around like a bloodhound. Suzan advised us that once we got her over there and she was looking around, to back off and let her go for the night. She assured us that 704 would find the calf. Then she told us to go back in the morning.

"The next day, I remember going up the hill and walking across the pasture and feeling incredibly guilty for causing this whole problem in the first place and then thinking, I hope they're together. It was just barely first light, and as I crossed the crest of the hill, I looked down across the road, and there was 704 standing with her calf, waiting for us," Jeff remembered, his face still registering amazement.

A happy ending for cow and newborn calf, thanks to two people who trusted my telepathic communication with 704 and her young one.

Honey and Laila

A beautiful Jersey cow named Honey enjoyed the visits by her friendly neighbor, Samantha, and now that Honey had a calf, Samantha came more often. But Samantha was concerned that Honey and her calf, Laila, were not being treated well.

"Over the last few years, Honey and I have developed a lovely friendship. In the past, I have expressed to my neighbor that I would love to purchase Honey and have her and Laila come live with me. They said no. But now, they're moving soon, so I may have another opportunity to try to make this happen.

"What I want to know is should I talk with her people again about coming to live here with me, or would she prefer for me not to interfere and let her go with her current owners, wherever that may be?" she asked.

"Honey and her calf love it when you visit and claim they have several human friends and caretakers. They both adore the land where they currently reside and, in some ways, would not like to move. However, they say the most important thing to know is that their current owners should decide. Honey says they are thinking about it now and may approach you about her staying.

"Honey showed me that her current people may make that decision *after* they have already moved her. She says it's also

58

important for her to express that she will be okay going with her people if that's what they decide. But she has loved your friendship, the serenity of just being together, and you coming with treats and happy thoughts to visit. She has a deep affection for your land as well," I said.

This beautiful honey-colored cow sent me a feeling and a picture of serenity on Samantha's land. She sent me the joy of her human friend's visit and how she introduced her new calf: from a little bit of a distance at first, but soon developing more trust in her.

Animals often have particular purposes for being with a specific human caretaker. Even in dangerous households, sometimes they want to stay because they are there to teach or to learn from their people. Seeing Honey not being cared for as she would have done it distressed Samantha. Letting them go is often a challenging request for sympathetic folks who have trouble seeing animals in less-than-ideal circumstances.

Candee

An emergency phone call from my long-time client and friend Jeff alerted me that his son's Holstein cow Candee was in trouble. Stuck in a creek that ran through his property, Candee waited. It was full of mud, and they asked me to let the cow know they would try and free her. They also asked if she had insight into why she had gotten stuck in the creek.

I'm way too smart to get myself stuck in the creek. There is something wrong with me physically, she said.

Jeff told me: "We worked to get her to stand up and couldn't get her on her feet, so we dragged her onto higher ground. She was still not able to stand up. We tried lifting her with hip clamps on the tractor. She would dangle there and stand with her front feet, but she would never stand on her rear legs. We moved her up to the corral for a few days and lifted her a few times each day, but she was never able to stand, so my son put her down after it became clear she was not going to recover."

The conclusion to this case was not what any of us wanted to happen, but Candee's admission that something was wrong did help to clarify things. None of the humans quite understood why this wise cow found herself in such a predicament, and Candee helped us understand her decline before the vet had an answer.

DOGS

10

Shepherd-Wolf Wyatt

Wyatt paced in circles around the tiny Tokyo apartment. He held his composure well for an 80-pound Northern Inuit dog, bred to look and howl like a wolf. His nature was gentle, but his world kept changing dramatically, and he was confused. And more than a little anxious.

Black, brown, and sable, this 5-year-old eye-catching canine looked exactly like what you would expect a German shepherd-wolf combination to look like: solid and striking.

The first thing Wyatt told me was that he tended to operate on instinct, and it was hard for him to be in such a restricted space under tight conditions. So, he paced all around the room, listening. He welcomed the guidance our conversation was about to provide on how to conduct himself in this apartment-sized space.

My territory has changed dramatically, and I feel so restricted. I share the concern and worry I feel in my people, he told me.

Wyatt was adopted by his human mom Suki when he was about a year old. Times were so different then. It was just the two of them. They went running, were constant companions, and he spent much time in nature. He loved rolling on the grass, breathing the fresh air, and chasing smaller animals in what he showed me was a great backyard.

What happened to my yard? He wondered. His world now included Suki's husband, a super-active toddler, and a tiny apartment in the busy, packed city.

Wyatt was one player in this consultation, but there were two others. Suki was a late 20's new mom, intelligent and responsible. Her young daughter, Hinata, was one of the most active 18-month-old girls I'd ever met. She was also in the room.

Little Hinata squirmed out of her mother's arms over and over and ran around the room. During the session, her toddler mood swung from exhilarated laughter to crying out in anger at being restrained. But when she was let loose, she went straight for the dog, pursuing him around the room, laughing gleefully. Wyatt continually retreated.

Generally, he told me, *it's best to steer clear of the child. I can't trust myself 100 percent not to react.*

My first question for Wyatt was urgent. Did he know what to do with a little person like Hinata? The proper answer coming back from a dog should be *I understand I am supposed to walk away from any assault and not defend myself*. But that's not what Wyatt said. And the baby's arm was already bandaged up from his bite.

To his credit, Wyatt tried repeatedly retreating, hiding behind the young mother. When things got tense, and he was about to defend himself against the child's constant pursuit, he knew enough to seek refuge behind Suki. But the baby often brought him toys and, in her babyness, beat him with said toys while this big dog tried to cope.

Recently, when Hinata straddled his sleeping body and pounced on him, he reacted out of instinct and bit her arm. And that explained the baby's bandaged arm.

"But I think they love each other," Suki said several times.

Wyatt had also bitten Suki's aging mother. He was sensitive to towel-drying, touching his feet or mouth, and several other areas of his body were hypersensitive. And no one had spent time desensitizing him in these areas. When I asked Suki if she could touch his snout to offer some T-Touch® healing, she said he wouldn't allow that.

She was afraid of his mouth, and so was the rest of her family, except for the baby, who unknowingly continued to provoke this anxious and suppressed dog.

Wyatt was big and strong and told me his exercise had been significantly curtailed once the baby came. He had lived with Suki's parents while the baby was growing up a bit, but now Suki had re-taken custody of her beloved dog.

"He's my responsibility," she said, feeling she could no

longer ask her parents to house him.

Meanwhile, his world shrank to apartment-sized, he lost his backyard, his mom was preoccupied, an unpredictable toddler had been added to the mix, and he was left to cope with an excess of energy in a small space. Wyatt was a city dog now; he was in his prime at five years old. His energy and need for speed, play, and exercise were at their peak.

Wyatt also had never had any actual boundaries. He had gone to training, but the techniques were no longer practiced once he got home. What he knew to do about the baby's mini-assaults was to try and hide, which wasn't working very well when they were in the same room. Suki kept them separate as much as possible, and she hoped animal communication could impress upon Wyatt the seriousness of the situation. Suki wanted him back full-time, but he had to promise not to bite anymore.

I gave the communication all I had. I knew this family was in danger. Suki's mother, the baby's grandmother, had already had surgery from Wyatt's bite, and the baby was still healing. And here was this powerful dog, confined to a small space, with a baby that was here, there, and everywhere—a recipe for further disaster.

"I want him to know how excruciating these injuries are, physically, emotionally, and psychologically," Suki emphasized. I wanted him to know that too. Badly.

I asked Wyatt if he understood what we were asking him to do, and he said yes, but he didn't think he could do it. He said he sometimes acted on instinct and couldn't guarantee that he would never react to a surprise stimulus. I told him that with babies, you could be dead as a log asleep, and one of them might come over, straddle your body, and start bouncing. Wyatt said he didn't think he could ignore such an unhappy surprise.

As the session continued, the baby toddled around the room in close pursuit of Wyatt, patting him, holding his muzzle between tiny hands, and shoving crackers toward his face. Wyatt continually circled behind Suki for retreat. And every 10 seconds or so, Suki scooped her daughter up to redirect her away from the powerful dog.

The Northern Inuit is said to be a good family dog, but what kind of family? The answer to that is one with *no* small children. Suki didn't have a small daughter when she became Wyatt's guardian. Her life had changed dramatically since then. This breed is also said to be excitable, although each animal is unique. Wyatt told me he couldn't guarantee that he wouldn't act out of instinct if he were hurt or startled. I'm not sure if that qualifies as 'excitable,' but there are some breeds that can ignore assault and others that can't.

Wyatt also possessed all of the admirable qualities a Northern Inuit is known for, including being friendly, gentle, calm, dependable, and familial.

Wyatt said straight out that he might bite again. The young mother, torn between protecting her loved ones and caring for her beloved dog, faced difficult decisions. This dilemma had no easy resolution.

67

Suki sent the dog back to her parents' house, where he had more room to roam. But during the same consultation, she decided to keep him in the small apartment and offer him much more exercise. Then Suki decided she couldn't do that, nor would she put her aging parents in another unsafe situation. When the consultation ended, she was still deciding.

Dangerous Dogs

I've met a few dogs over thousands of consultations that bit people. Some felt they needed a little more time and precise guidance, while others thought they might not make it as a good domestic companion in this lifetime. Too much damage and trauma made aggression a sure thing for some dogs. Others weren't wired to flow through trauma without reacting.

A few dogs that knew they would be euthanized were matter-of-fact about understanding that biting was unacceptable, but they couldn't stop defending themselves.

I guess I'm just not going to make it as a domestic companion this time around, they've said.

It's understandable but heartbreaking when the undeniable choices are re-home, re-train, or in some cases, euthanize your beloved animal friend. No dog chooses being restrained for a lifetime or never seeing the sunshine again in that situation.

Just in Time

In this case, a neighbor who lived next door in Suki's apartment complex became a bit of an angel. He loved Wyatt and wanted to help. He was an athletic man who took Wyatt running at least twice daily. Because of her continuing concerns, Suki first allowed Wyatt to stay next door for overnight visits. But soon, he was living next door with the far more suitable single running man and getting all of the outdoor time he needed to be more balanced.

The beauty of the situation unfolded when Wyatt told me how many people cared for him. He said his family had expanded to include this athletic man next door and felt relaxed and well-exercised. He no longer had the baby to dodge, but he could visit her and the other parts of his previous neighborhood family, including Suki and her husband.

11

Solving A Shocking Mystery

At first glance, the photo of Flo told me she was a highly sensitive dog. In my mind's eye, she winced and withdrew almost imperceptibly as I tuned in to begin our meeting. She was with her human companion, Marie. It was December, and a heavy blanket of snow had fallen in Missouri, where the woman and her jet-black dog, cozily tucked in, sat next to an efficient woodstove for our phone session.

Flo's photo showed her sweet dog face. She had the head of a black Labrador retriever, but her body was more prolonged, smaller, and slimmer than a purebred Labrador. Her huge brown eyes looked a little sad and a whole lot shy. I felt the depth of her soul through her gaze, and a knowing washed over me that this was the kind of dog that would crumble under corporal punishment. I felt a deep sense that even a raised voice could crush the spirit of this tender soul.

I'd already connected with Spirit before our phone session began, so I telepathically added Flo to the conversation. Marie completed our three-entity workgroup. As I connected, the signs and symbols of PTSD started playing in my head. I took note, then put the information into my mind's sidebar area as Marie began telling me why she'd called.

"Flo's brother Kam passed away last month, and she seemed to be doing surprisingly well afterward. She was present when he passed. But I've enjoyed our one-on-one time," she told me.

"Around the time of the Covid-19 shutdown, I began to work from home. I'm a psychotherapist, and I was doing mainly video sessions and still seeing a few clients in my office. I found a new dog walker and daycare, and Flo seemed to enjoy that, happy to leave each day with them," she explained.

"But as the weeks progressed, I noticed mysterious symptoms and behaviors. Flo began licking her lips and stress yawning. She wasn't sleeping as soundly, and she was having difficulty getting comfortable," she said.

Marie had been to a veterinarian, and none of the vet's tests showed any ailments the doctor could pinpoint. All were listed as "unremarkable," which led her to believe the issue was psychological, so she looked for answers and solutions via animal communication.

As I stayed linked to Flo, images of her fear and flinching came through. The feeling of PTSD persisted, so I went through a list of symptoms, asking about which ones Flo was experiencing. She nailed it down to this list:

- Recurrent, unwanted distressing memories of the traumatic event.

- Reliving the traumatic event as if it were happening again (flashbacks).

- Upsetting dreams or nightmares about the traumatic event.

- Severe distress about something that reminded her of the traumatic event.

- Avoidance of people's touch.

- Fear of activities she had once enjoyed, like riding in the car.

"If I go to pet Flo, she often flinches. I must be very gentle, wait for her head to drop down, and then I can pet her. Flo's greatest sensitivity is her neck, and any fast movement towards her head startles her. Sometimes she will even squeal as if it hurts," she explained.

Marie had already been working with a remote healer from the Netherlands, who she reported had helped relieve some of Flo's symptoms. But she wanted to know what she could do going forward to support the dog in returning to a more peaceful state of mind.

These feelings from Flo were some I'd felt a few times before, and I searched my sensory banks for a match. But we soon discovered why the dog had turned skittish and fearful.

The source of Flo's continuing angst was a recent rattlesnake training done with a shock collar. According to the trainer, it was the lowest possible setting for the electrical collar. The symptoms were not apparent as a problem for a couple of days. So connecting the dots took time.

Being electrocuted triggered Flo's PTSD. She exhibited typical symptoms, including flashbacks, nightmares, severe anxiety, and uncontrollable thoughts of electricity passing through her head and neck. Flo's PTSD also included avoidance of collars and human hands and negative changes in physical and emotional reactions like cowering. It was a terrifying event.

I worked on remote healing for Flo's neck and head, and I was glad there was another healer on the job with me from across the world. Marie and I talked about collars that vibrate and emit a beeping sound instead, but once she surrendered Flo to the snake aversion training, she consented to their techniques. These shock techniques seem to be effective in keeping dogs far away from snakes, but there are better ways that don't hurt or traumatize the animal.

Frida Freaks

Another one of my dog clients, Frida, was a tiny 1.5-year-old terrier mix that experienced similar trauma. She was all ears that pointed to the sides, making her black and brown head look a tad like baby Yoda, and she was reeling from the results of rattlesnake training that involved an electric collar. Frida was still getting used to an entirely new environment when the exercise happened, just a few days after a lengthy car ride. And that car ride was at the end of a stressful time of uprooting from Northern California, then relocating to Arizona. Everything was so unpredictable!

I'm not a good traveler, was the message she sent me, along with the nausea of motion sickness.

"Do you understand that your person is a traveler? She's on the road all the time," I said. Her human mom, Mary, was a good friend I'd known for at least three decades.

No, Frida said, and I was puzzled for a minute, then I realized she was right. My friend, a wanderer by nature, had stayed put for several years, and Frida had not traveled with her much. But recently, Mary had retired, and the two set off for new digs in Arizona. My friend had put her traveling shoes on again, and Frida was still getting her bearings in the new house. New smells and new wildlife had her on alert.

Whenever I get into the car, bad things happen, she told me. Pictures of vet visits came through, then the sickening motion of the vehicle, images whizzing by the windows, and a feeling as if my feet were no longer on solid ground.

But most recently, a terrible thing happened. Frida said she had been dropped off at a place she didn't know, and a person unfamiliar to her had control of her leash. She was tentatively moving through this new desert landscape, and Mary, whom she trusted, was nowhere to be found.

Sniffing the ground, she caught the scent of something unfamiliar, and suddenly, wham! An electrical current ran through her neck, throat, and head, then down her whole body, and boy, did that hurt! It was an 8 out of 10 on the pain scale, and it took several minutes for her to compose herself. She looked for places to hide but was in unfamiliar territory. She could touch her footpads onto the earth's surface, which helped, but she was knocked off her delicate center by the current that zapped her petite body.

When I smell that scent now, I shake and shiver, she showed me a few weeks later. *I'm terrified. But I make a wide berth around the scent. Before this, I did not associate the snake with a problem. I was curious about it.*

"I'm so sorry it was so painful and frightening," I told her. "This is how we try to keep you safe from poisonous snakes."

Then I offered a distance healing for the trauma that caused her etheric body to shiver as we spoke of the incident. Frida still has anxiety attacks when she gets into the car, but she accepted the healing I had to offer.

Frida and Mary reached a greater understanding as a result of our session. The little dog understood she came together with her traveling human to become more flexible. And her human realized that Frida is sometimes quite content at home, just waiting for her return.

Shocking Collars

A shock collar looks like a standard one with a small box outfitted with two metal electrodes. Electrodes are designed to penetrate fur and press directly against the skin. The collar's electrodes often burn the neck. Between 1500 to 4500 volts of electricity are delivered through a painful shock to the animal. Voltage information is often hidden or obscured, so some collars may operate at higher voltages.

Why not try the shock collar yourself before using it on an animal? Does the thought make you quiver? Thankfully, you can see what happens without trying it out yourself because several humans have already done that on YouTube. Check it out.

Some people who try out the collar on-camera report the pain level is an 8 out of 10. Some are left writhing on the ground at the lowest levels of electrical current from the collar. Even those who set out to prove the collar is not so bad seem traumatized and have reversed course. Trying out the electronic shock collar is an event they'll never forget. Dogs don't forget that kind of trauma, either

Misuse of shock collars is not uncommon, partly due to a lack of clear instructions. At a field trial event in Maine, Green Acres Kennel (greenacreskennel.com) staff witnessed a life-altering event for one particular dog. They wrote about it in their article The Unintended Consequences of Shock Collars: https://www.greenacreskennel.com/information/articles/dog-behavior-and-training/689-the-unintended-consequences-of-shock-collars.

"A dog owner with two dogs was working with one of his

dogs and had a second dog in its crate. The dog that he was working with did not respond to a command, so the owner pressed a button on the remote to shock the dog. The dog still did not respond to the command, so the owner shocked the dog again. This happened three times. Meanwhile, the dog in the crate was yelping each time the owner was intending to shock the dog he was working with. It was not until our staff member pointed it out that the owner realized he was shocking his dog in the crate and not the one he was working with." The owner was using the wrong remote unit.

In my practice, this might play out with folks coming to me for a session, wanting to know why their new rescue dog is paranoid about getting into a crate; why they can't stand to have anything near their neck; why their ears are ultrasensitive; or why they shake their heads all the time. When a dog has this kind of experience, it's not unusual for his behavior to become illogical, fearful, aggressive, or unpredictable. Dogs who are shocked often turn on the people who are shocking them or become aggressive when they've never exhibited aggression before.

"A study published in 2000 looked at five dogs who were subjected to shock collar containment systems and who later bit people, resulting in a lawsuit. No dog had a prior history of displaying aggression towards people, and it is believed that the dogs received a shock at the time of the attack. There is no evidence to suggest that the humans bitten were acting in a threatening manner before the attack. *In all cases, the dogs bit the victim repeatedly and uninhibitedly, resulting in serious bodily injury.*

"Other studies on the use of electrical shock on other species, including humans, have noted the extreme

viciousness and intensity of shock-elicited aggression." 2
Polsky, Richard, (2000), Can Aggression in Dogs Be Elicited
Through the Use of Electronic Pet Containment Systems?
Journal of Applied Animal Welfare Science, 3(4), 345-357,
http://www.dogexpert.com/wp-content/uploads/2012/05/
Electronic-fences.pdf.

Reward-Based Training

The good news is that studies show that positive
reinforcement is just as effective as shock aversion.
Source: https://www. companionanimalpsychology.com/
2013/06/the-end-for-shock-collars.html

Alternatives to using a shock collar include a reward-
based training program and more effective management
of your dog. Clicker and reward-based training make for
a confident working or performance dog. Take a look at
the U.S. Navy for the effectiveness of positive
reinforcement methods. The Navy has trained some of the
most talented working animals in the world exclusively
with reward-based training.

I've met hundreds of dogs in my practice who have
benefited from positive reinforcement or rewards-based
training. In many cases, I've consulted with confused
animals who thought they were doing what their people
wanted them to do when the opposite was true.

Dodger was a 3-year-old dog with a square head like a
boxer and funny ears that were pointed straight forward
and folded over in the same direction. He had a brown
body with a black muzzle and a few spots of black on his
tongue. His shrill, continuous whine pierced the ears of
his human family and kept everyone in the house on
edge. So John called me for help.

It's confusing, said Dodger. *I don't get the idea that I'm not supposed to be ramped up.*

With that, he showed me he was held, kissed, and cuddled when he whined. His human was saying, "it's alright, it's alright," and he was getting the idea that it was. It was alright to whine, be amped up, focus on the mail carrier, freak out at cars going by, and vocalize loudly at any happening inside or outside the house. All of these activities got him affection and attention.

John, his person, was coached to find times, even if for a fleeting moment, to praise and reward Dodger with affection whenever he was sleepy, napping, or super calm. It didn't take long for Dodger to re-wire his anxious brain. He was an intelligent dog whose currency was affection, so it also made sense for John to withdraw all attention from the whining he didn't want and physically turn his back on it until it stopped.

I asked John to change his behavior since Dodger felt confused. John was to turn his back on Dodger and keep turning his back until the moment when he caught the dog calm or quiet. Then he turned around to offer praise or affection to Dodger when he calmed. It worked like a charm. Dodger didn't take long to get the message: quiet was rewarded, and anxiety was ignored. It didn't take long, but it did take consistency.

Positive reinforcement utilizes teaching techniques that reward desired behaviors instead of punishing unwanted behavior.
Positive rewards reduce a dog's anxiety, anger, and frustration experienced with punishment-based models of training.

Rewards-based training leads to a more confident, connected animal companion.

When an animal's behavior is guided by an offering of happy rewards like praise, treats, or affection, trust in their human companion deepens, they make more eye contact, keep their heads high, and have far less stress in the body. On the other hand, threatening treatment erodes the tender trust between humans and animals.

12

Thanks, But No Thanks

Hiking the dry, brown hills of San Luis Obispo with a neighbor I'd just met for the first time was the start of an adventure with a dog out on his own. Margie had come to my front door 15 minutes earlier and knocked.

"Are you the one that's the animal whisperer?" Margie asked me. I told her I was, and she asked if I could go with her to see a dog that she and other neighbors had been feeding. There were questions, namely, what was this dog's story? And would he agree to go with her to find a home with people? She was willing to help, and it was vital to let him know she had the best intentions.

Wolfie was an Akita who lived on the outskirts of a ranch, and he said it was the perfect place for him. A neutered male who lost his home to conflict, he showed me he'd been living with a couple and their young child. He was mostly loyal to the female head of the household, and he showed me that the male half of the couple wasn't very fond of him.

I barked at the man a few times when he was yelling at the woman and acting in a threatening manner, Wolfie showed me. The man scowled at him from that day forward and looked for a reason to get rid of the dog. The opportunity presented itself when their baby boy was about 3 years old.

Wolfie was lying down, and the toddler came to straddle him, joyfully jumping up and down on his spine. The dog turned around toward the child and barked once, frightening the child, who began to cry loudly. The incident gave the dad the ammunition he needed to advocate for getting rid of the dog. He planned to take him to a kill-type shelter, but the woman felt he would never be adopted and intervened.

The man issued an ultimatum, "Either you get rid of the dog, or I will." The young woman was distraught but had to allow her husband to deal with the problem. He set Wolfie loose near an open area where there were dozens of squirrels and other animals to hunt. In the distance, about 1,000 feet away, there was also a large barn.

The hills where Wolfie lived now were wide open. He could see anything coming his way for a mile, and he made sure to trot in the opposite direction when Margie and the other folks who left food for him came. I had a large and lovingly-selected bone for him and other good food, but Wolfie parked himself a hundred yards away as we left him the food. My conversation with the big Akita occurred on the mountain where he lived.

Wolfie informed me that construction had come to the area where he camped. Workers of different kinds offered him food, but they also attempted to trap him. He had busted out of a carrier and thus came to associate food with entrapment. Eventually, he came to accept food offerings, but he only ate it after the humans were out of sight, at a distance, or under cover of darkness.

Concerned neighbors supplied the Akita with an Igloo doghouse, but he was not much inclined toward any confinement and said his fur coat served him well. He also had a tent-like structure built for him which he liked because he could see out of both ends and get out quickly and easily. He said he might use it in a rainstorm.

I did a body scan which revealed that Wolfie had a bit of arthritis but still had very keen senses of hearing and smell. He was on high alert to changes in his environment and enjoyed the other animals that lived out in the pasture, mainly from a distance. There was a peaceful communion among the animals: *Live and let live.*

He said he had plenty to eat, could use a little oil for his skin (occasional tuna with fish oil, maybe once a week), and used the large bones to dislodge a tooth if it hurt. This big dog had no desire to take up with a permanent human or live in a city-type environment. He was content keeping his distance and living out his life as a dog with many non-masters. The woman who had asked for my help accepted his answers.

"If you change your mind about having another household, this is a good woman to partner with," I told him, and he filed the information away.

A few years later, Wolfie disappeared. His final message: *I gave myself to another animal for its food and survival. I loved participating in the turn of the wheel of life. When I was done using it, my body served a good purpose.*

13

Unjust Rewards

On an autumn day in early November, I met with Charlotte, who had a problem with her chihuahua, Brinx, going after one of the cats in the house. Brinx was calm around two of the cats, but the third one, Mia, was fearful, and it set up a scenario where the diminutive dog was sharply focused on her, waiting for a good chase.

To make matters worse, Brinx was a young 2-year-old rescue with no domestic training nor any idea what it meant to be a good companion animal. As a breeding dog, he had spent most of his life in kennels with minimal human interaction. Now he was free of cages and confinement, curiously delighted to explore his new home and his new life.

I'm fascinated with this black cat, Mia. She hisses and scratches, but I still want to get closer. When I first got here, I barked loudly right in Mia's face to let her know I would defend myself, and my human mom was fine with that. She encourages me to be hostile to

Mia. Brinx sent pictures and feelings to convey this message, and I soon understood his point of view.

Charlotte had tried to fix the problem, but inadvertently she was rewarding the dog with affection and putting the cat at greater risk. Every day, Charlotte took the dog in her arms, found the cat on her carpeted tree in her safe room, and saying, "kiss, kiss," thrust Brinx's face directly into Mia's face. The cat hissed, jumped up, and ran. The dog tried to look away, growled and squirmed, and Charlotte told me, "It's as if he's saying, 'No, I don't want to kiss, kiss,' but I force him, saying, 'Yes, you *will* kiss.'"

Charlotte didn't understand how she was rewarding the dog, and I explained to her that Brinx got cuddles and affection when she picked him up and held him, and she did this when he was overly focused on the cat, reinforcing the razor-sharp intensity. The dog terrorized Mia, and the hostility and aggression between them accelerated. Mia felt as if nowhere was safe anymore.

I'm a curious guy with a ton of energy, Brinx told me, *and I need to run, run, run. I am full of youthful exuberance, and it is focused on the chase when it is unexpressed. This scared cat draws me in when I can't chase a squirrel or a bird,* he relayed to me.

Mia had been barricaded alone in a separate room for many months, where she spent most of her life. When I asked Mia if she could expect her human mom Charlotte to protect her, she said no.

Mia was eight weeks old when Charlotte adopted her from the shelter, and she was about six months old at the time of this session. She was frightened then, too. But the cat's fears were amplified when Charlotte adopted the unsocialized Brinx. The dog had been with Charlotte for four months when our session took place.

"I need Mia to stand up for herself and stop being afraid of the new dog. I want her to please come out of the bedroom," Charlotte said.

When I told Mia, she said *I need more vertical space to feel safe. If Charlotte wants me to join the rest of the animals in the living room, I'll need to be up high where the dog can't reach,* she told me.

I explained to Charlotte how important it is for a cat to be up very high, preferably close to the ceiling. I related what it felt like to tune into a cat up in the corner of a room. The feeling of relief and safety when the two walls come together behind you is comforting. When it's possible to see the whole room, and nothing can get to where you are before you have a chance to get away, that feels feline safe.

"She's not allowed on the counters, but I might be able to clear off the bookcase for her," Charlotte said.

"That would be a great start," I told her.

"All Brinx does is stare at that room where Mia is hiding. Mia stays under a chair where the dog can't see her. I need Mia to understand not to be afraid of Brinx. They must get along, or the dog has to go back to the shelter," she said.

I gave Charlotte a few more tips on interrupting the focus Brinx had on the cat and the room where she liked to hide. Then I suggested to Mia that she was a confident cat and could take the upper hand in the situation. The conversation I had with both animals included Charlotte's desire for a peaceful, calm home and Brinx taking his young attention outside to run and play instead of being focused and frozen, waiting for the cat to make a move.

Three cats and another dog are now all part of your pack, I told Brinx. I let him know that this cat, Mia, was included. I sent him pictures of protecting the cat instead of chasing her.

Charlotte, a lady in her 70s, said she would work on finding ways for this young pup to express his exuberant and playful energy. Brinx also said it would help if he could go outside and chase wildlife, which seemed like a great solution.

Things had changed when I checked with Charlotte a few weeks later. She'd stopped her morning "face to face" with the animals, which helped immensely. And there were other changes, too.

"It was so amazing," she said. "Brinx took himself outside to run after squirrels and rabbits. He would stand at the door and wait; my fenced backyard was perfect. He has stopped focusing on the bedroom door, and Mia has come out of the room and joined us. I cleaned off the bookcase, and she loves it up there."

New household configurations or new animal companions are a common issue in my practice. First, uncovering, then healing past traumas or present relationship issues is part of that process. It's very gratifying when things become more harmonious, and people can immediately see a change in the animal's behavior. The animal kingdom is almost always happy to oblige, and it inspires me in my work and moves my heart to gladness to be a part of this miracle.

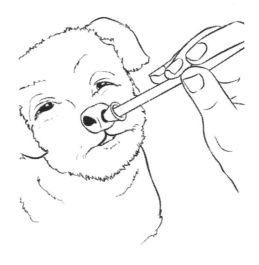

14

Residual Wallop

It was raining, and I loved it. It was my kind of California winter: refreshing and renewing. The rain, fog, and wind reassured me that I lived in the best place on earth. Until summertime, when California demanded we realize she has a semi-arid climate. Then temperatures tiptoed over 100 degrees, especially in the valleys. I retreated inside quickly anytime the thermometer hit 85 degrees.

But not today. The glorious rain came down, and we rejoiced. My day began with meditation and a quiet opening to receive the message coming from my first clients: a dog named Manny and his person Andrea.

Expanding into the Highest Good, I found my sacred

connection to this small elder dog and opened the door to communicating. His little head was reeling, and his tiny deep brown eyes were watery. Moisture trails slid down the side of Manny's small snout. His person began.

"Did something happen at the kennel? I want to know what he needs from me. Is he saying goodbye? Should I take him to a vet, or does he need to rest and recover?" Andrea fired questions one after another in rapid succession.

As my consciousness melded into Manny's, I felt tired and struggled to breathe. Andrea said he had stage 4 congestive heart failure. At stage 3 of this disease, fatigue, shortness of breath, coughing, and wheezing are part of an everyday struggle to draw the next breath. But I felt there was something else. Something from which Manny could recover. I knew this little dog was not ready to leave his body. Parts of Manny were still very puppy-like.

There's something in my nose, he showed me. *It's wet and uncomfortable, and I feel like I'm drowning.*

"We gave him Bordetella in his nose the other day and sent him to a kennel for one night with our other two dogs," Andrea explained.

I feel as if I'm recovering from a very nasty wallop that hit my body like a freight train, Manny said.

That made all kinds of sense to me because the Bordetella vaccine can produce life-threatening side effects in some dogs. Many vets won't administer the vaccine when a dog is in stage 4 of congestive heart failure due to the compromised system. Swelling of the face and red splotches or hives on the stomach and chest are common effects.

So, Manny was recovering. His body struggled with the CHF, and this vaccine zapped his remaining energy and made his head swim. As I checked in with his body, it felt like he had influenza.

"We came back, and he was so excited to see us. He started gasping, and now he's just laying here calmly wheezing as he breathes," Andrea said. "His body feels hot, and he threw up a little bit last night."

I'm not dying right now, and I think I will recover from this, although there are a lot of other issues in my body, Manny told me.

Manny was still eating and drinking. Most of the time, he felt quite content, he said, except when he had trouble breathing. But he knew it was all part of the process of an aging body. His struggling body was now assimilating the vaccine, the wallop he'd mentioned earlier. It was a lot to process through a barely functioning liver.

I marveled at Manny's tolerance and continued joy with his people. His calm countenance felt like profound grace and gratitude. He didn't blame anyone. He knew his people were trying to follow the rules of the kennel and keep him safe from kennel cough.

I encouraged Andrea to spend time being fully present with Manny in the difficult days ahead and to carefully consider the use and administration of vaccines from now on in Manny's advanced senior years.

15

Hi Ho, Silver: Are You Happy?

"I would like to ask her how she feels about her life with me. Is there anything bothering her? Anything that she needs or would like? Any way I could make her life better and happier?" asked Hattie, who dearly loved her compact, muscular herding dog, Silver.

Silver's name referred partly to her beautiful silver, black, and grey coat. I opened the portal to receive her communication, and she took me back to when out of a litter of puppies, she was the chosen one. She wanted me to know about her beginnings with this family first.

I made it very clear that I was the one this man should pick. There were lots of other puppies, she showed me, *but I played with him and won him over.*

Hattie confirmed that when they adopted Silver, her husband bonded with the dog and chose her to come home with them.

I asked Silver to show me more highlights of her time with her beloved humans and what made her happy. She was a Queensland Heeler and showed me she had what every cattle dog wants: cattle!

I was so happy for her. I felt a sense of pride and fulfillment coming from her, and I quickly assumed that she had a job as a herding dog. But an assumption in animal communication is never a good thing, so I asked her how she interacted with the cattle.

I'm not really into herding them, she sent to me, *but I like having them around anyway as animal friends. Every now and then, I get into the herding mood with them, but they don't always play that game with me. Sometimes, they just get annoyed.*

I had to chuckle at her picture, but I congratulated myself for checking my assumptions about this herding dog expressing how happy she was to have cattle!

"That's right," Hattie confirmed. "She doesn't herd them. They're mostly in the pasture."

"What else makes you happy?" I asked Silver.

Being outdoors and doing plenty of running, she showed me. *I would not be a good 'apartment dog.' I need to be outside in nature.*

"It looks like she's showing me a picture of hiking, going into the woods with her humans, and camping. These are activities she loves. Any way you could make her life better? The more time you can spend in physical activity, the better. She does like to go places, even though she has a difficult time with the movement of the car," I said.

"We are a hiking and camping family and have spent lots of time in those scenes," said Hattie, "but I was going to ask you about her discomfort in the car. She hunkers down low in the floorboards. What's that about?"

"Silver has some motion sickness," I said, and we explored a couple of herbal remedies. "Silver feels nauseated when the car moves. She needs quiet and dark. Having the 'room' move makes her feel seasick. There are several things you can do. Put black paper on the car windows in the back or put her in a crate where she can't see the outside. Perform T-Touch® Mouthwork for dogs before you get into the car. It helps reduce anxiety, it's free and very effective, and there's a video on my website to show you how."

Our second inquiry was related to Silver's health. Although I do not diagnose or treat illness, there are things I can do as an animal communicator to report how an animal's body is feeling. My services are designed to complement veterinary care, but I can tell if a particular food or medication feels rough in a specific animal's body.

"Her health in general has been great. She had limber tail once, a year or so ago, and that's about it, apart from a few broken nails here and there that sometimes give her trouble," Hattie reported.

I asked Silver if I could scan her body, and she offered her permission.

"What I can feel is a digestive issue. Are you seeing loose or hard stools? I'm getting the message that she could use more protein from meat and vegetables. She is a curious dog and loves to see new things in her bowl. Some of the greens I see in the bowl are colors coming from vegetables like carrots, peas, potatoes, sweet potatoes, and broccoli. Try her on some fresh meats and veggies.

"As an omnivore, she will need about 65% protein. (That's according to Dr. Pitcairn's book, Natural Health for Dogs and Cats, a wonderful resource.) Try both steamed and raw veggies, which should comprise about 30% of her diet. Carrots keep coming up as a potential reward or catching game. Small bits of carrot are a great snack. The 'limber tail syndrome' feels related to a lot of tension there, where the tail meets the body," I told her. I recommended another method for relieving the tension stored at the head of Silver's tail.

Hattie wanted to explore her relationship with Silver since she felt an ancient connection to her dog. "She's been a huge force of positive transformation in my life. Please tell her how deeply grateful I am to her for everything she has taught me and all the healing she has brought to my life. I love her so dearly," she said.

"You've been together before during a time when she was your horse companion, and you were a grand lady. The scene has a medieval flavor, and the relationship is extremely close, as close as any dog companion might be today in the sense of going everywhere with their person. You relied on her for many things like freedom, companionship, and solace, and she looked out for your safety. She also had an affection for her human dad at that time and shows him as a suitor who protected his lady," I said.

In some ways, this session with Silver and Hattie might be called typical, except that there's no such thing as predictive or routine when it comes to what the animals will say. But the inquiry Hattie made into finding out whether she could make her dog's life happier *is* a typical inquiry and one I'm glad to address in facilitating these profound connections.

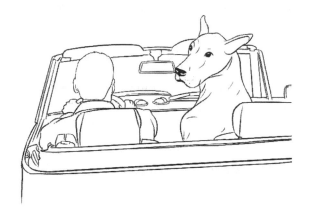

16

Ollie's Match

Ollie looked out from the metal bars of his kennel, and with a slight turn of his bulldog-like head, he caught the eye of animal shelter volunteer Lucia. A combination of inquiry and goofy comedy radiated from his black face, topped off by perfectly coiffed white eyebrows. Another thinner white line divided the top of his snout symmetrically. The line spread left and right where his black nose began, making it look like white eyeliner defining the top of his nose. Ollie's face was uniquely branded with a lookalike of the automaker Tesla's iconic "T" symbol.

Lucia was there to take another dog out for a walk, but this 9-year-old puppy-like Boxer/Great Dane mix captured her attention so thoroughly that she took him out instead. He was charming like that. And his silliness always got the girl.

Ollie was tall, elevated high on spindly legs. *It's an excellent height to be since it's perfect for getting rubbed on and petted*, he showed me.

"How are you feeling being in the shelter?" I asked him.

Fantastic, he said. *I've never met a person I didn't like, and right now I'm waiting for my new person. I'm not at all discouraged*, Ollie explained telepathically. *This shelter is a good place, and people care. I'm not happy about the confinement or the anxious animals, but I know it's temporary, at least for me. Meanwhile, I'm a staff favorite!*

Lucia called me to facilitate a session with Ollie and to find out if they were a good match. Unbeknownst to me, Lucia had made her decision already, but she wanted information on what might challenge her new companion and confirmation of the things she thought she knew already.

"How do you like your name?" I asked him because Lucia reported that he did not respond to his name.

Sir Otis is so formal, he said, *and I am a more comical, casual type guy. But I have a suggestion. How about Ollie?*

"How would you feel about being Lucia's companion? Living with her and being her dog friend for life?" I asked.

I can't wait, he said enthusiastically.

He was ready to go. He said his higher purpose was to bring joy and that the name change had been super helpful in having people recognize him for his whimsy.

Two months later, Lucia told me, "He responded to the name immediately. He's been with me a few months, and he's delightful. My vet confirmed that Ollie's probably nine years

102

old but acts like a nine-month-old. He has a puppy personality and loves to play. Aside from separation anxiety, he has been a perfect pooch. He rescued me."

Lucia also had some questions for Ollie, and the first was how he felt about other animals, particularly dogs. She wanted to know if Ollie wanted a companion animal to keep him company when she went out. He seemed to have separation anxiety, and she thought it might help.

Ollie showed me he did not trust all dogs and that he'd been attacked by an out-of-balance dog before. He wasn't sure how to discriminate between a good dog and an aggressive dog until it was too late. And he had been a very trusting soul at one time.

He *did* think a cat would be good company. He pictured the cat as a long-haired tabby at least six years old—a calm, cool, collected cat.

"That's an interesting idea," said Lucia. "I would never have thought of that."

With the companionship question for him settled, Lucia told me that Ollie loved people and became overly excited whenever there was a knock on the door. She wanted me to ask him to calm down when visitors came. I felt his over-the-top excitement in my bones and learned that he trusted people more than he trusted dogs. I also gave Lucia a few pointers on how to calm him down when people came over.

Lucia and Ollie were a match made *in* heaven and *through* a local shelter where heavenly matches are often made. Ollie was one of several dogs who have told me the animal shelter was a wonderful place where regular meals were served, and the people there cared deeply about the well-being of their animal charges.

Ollie was a meticulous listener and a conscientious dog dedicated to his new human companion. She knew the communication was honest because his behavior had changed. Ollie said yes to all of our requests leading to greater harmony in Lucia's home: what she'd hoped for when she made her appointment. I was grateful to him for his outstanding communication skills and for participating with us in this grand adventure.

17

Territorial Insecurity

Clayton, a mini-cockapoo living in a 2-dog household, became my client in the spring of 2020. (The mini cockapoo is a cute, smaller version of a dog that is half cocker spaniel and half poodle.) Clayton's people wanted me to talk to him about peeing in the house.

The young family consisted of Brad, his wife Leah, and their dogs, Clayton and Dexie.

My territory has been invaded, and I'm not quite sure what is mine anymore, he said. *I don't know how to protect my people when I am inside at night and numerous other animals are outside. I'm not sure what to do, so I claim* all *of the inside territory,* he showed me.

Territorial insecurity is a common issue I deal with, and I wanted to clarify the extent of the threat, so I asked him if it was inside or out.

It's both inside and out, he said, sending me telepathic pictures of animals roaming around outside at night in a place he didn't know well. New kinds of unfamiliar wildlife moved around under the house and underground, and he was acutely aware of their movement via smell and sense. There were animals everywhere in this new place, and he wasn't sure what he should do about it.

How do I protect my people from animals outside when I can't get out there? He wanted to know.

I showed him that his scent outdoors would be adequate to anchor his claim and negotiated with Brad and Leah to take him around the front and back yards to relieve himself.

One thing was still a mystery to me. I didn't understand why "home" seemed so unfamiliar to him, so I asked his people.

"We've just moved into a new house. Been here about three months," Brad told me.

This consultation included conversations with Clayton about a new way to protect his people by marking outside. I let him know that the animals outside would not be a threat while he was inside. I also reiterated that animals eliminating inside the house was a mighty big problem for their human companions.

He felt much better after our consultation. I'm happy to say that his people did their homework by spreading his scent all around the periphery of the new place, and the problem of Clayton relieving himself in the house did not happen again.

When behavior changes completely and immediately

106

following a session, the results of animal communication is clear, present, and very satisfying. I'm grateful to Clayton for his willingness to make changes as a result of our exchanges.

18

Doki Loves Digging

Some consultations involve a body scan of the animal, a very informative technique I use often. The focused consciousness moves along the body until it stops, at which point I'm asked to look deeper. Telepathic communication can detect conditions like blockages, congestion, inflammation, fatigue, and even parasitic invasions. I've mentioned before that animal communication is no substitute for veterinary care, but I can sense areas where more inquiry is appropriate.

Doki, a very young Cavalier King Charles Spaniel, had digestive issues, specifically chronic diarrhea. The pup had just been switched to super high-quality dog food, so I wondered if he was still integrating the new food. When I asked Doki what he thought might help, he showed me pictures of oatmeal in his food bowl; for me, that's a call for a bland diet.

An animal communication specialist can feel what your animal feels and report it to you, which is the crux of this translation practice. And the feeling I translated was that Doki felt sluggish. As I began the body scan, my attention started at the tip of Doki's nose and moved slowly through the snout. It skidded to a stop when I got to the belly of this 12-week-old puppy and zoomed in like a camera lens.

I requested that Doki's people go over the ingredient list of his current food with me. They read each ingredient of the new food as I looked for allergens with a technique I use akin to muscle testing. It's simply a psychic inquiry into the body's reaction to certain ingredients.

Telepathically, I put each new food ingredient through the little dog's body to see how it reacted. With this procedure, the body brightens up, goes dull, or stays the same, signifying how it's responding to the ingredient.

The first ingredient on the label was chicken. Chicken is a wholesome protein in most cases, so I was surprised Doki's body barely registered it on the good side of the scale. To me, that meant Doki was either slightly allergic to poultry or another phenomenon was operating: the chicken processed for dog food in Doki's bowl had been inhumanely treated before becoming animal food. I find more and more that animals used in food but treated inhumanely don't provide much nutritional support. I reported that and went on to the next ingredient until we covered half a dozen or so.

My human client Humari had other compelling questions for Doki, whose name meant "heart flutter" in his person's native language, Japanese. Here's our conversation:

Humari: How can we improve as your human family?

Doki: *There is nothing my human family would not do for me. I'm thoroughly spoiled in their view.*

Humari: What are you enjoying about being with our family?

Doki: *The joy I bring. We all have lots of fun together.*

Humari: What did you come to earth this lifetime to learn?

Doki: *To learn to be in a body like this one. I'm not used to being this small or this earth-bound.*

Humari: What and where were you before this lifetime?

Doki: *I was a hawk. Very free, flying in the air. Responsible for myself. I am learning how to be dependent on humans, a scary proposition. I used to be in charge of my food supply, shelter, and health.*

Humari: Do you know what is causing your loose stools, and do you have ideas or preferences as to how to help you?

Doki shows me an image of oatmeal in his bowl.

Humari: How is your body feeling? Are there any issues?

Doki: *Sluggish. I need protein, but this new food will help. I need a bland diet for a day or two. Rice and broth.*

Humari: What do you want us to know about what it is like to be a dog?

Doki: *Being a small dog differs from being a medium-sized or large dog.*

(See the Sidebar for an exercise I recommended to humans to understand this feeling on a deeper level.)

Humari: How can we make the crate more pleasant for you?

Doki: *I'm bouncing off the walls in there. Leave the door open.*

Humari: What motivates you most to learn new skills and behaviors?

Doki: *Not food but affection.*

Humari: What is your favorite activity?

Doki: *Digging.*

Humari: I hate that. I can't stand it when you dig. What makes you want to dig?

Doki: *It makes me so very happy. How can we work it out?*

Humari: How can I help you to eat out of your food bowl without me hand feeding you?

Doki: *It's nice when you do, but I won't go hungry if you stop.*

Humari asked if she could also thank Doki for behaviors he had figured out at his young age. She sent this list of messages that I passed along to him:

- Thank you for coming to our family.

- Thank you for your kind sweetness.

- Thank you for pooping only outside.

- Thank you for not barking.

- Thank you for being quiet in your crate.

- Thank you for your patience.

Then she asked me to go over the house rules with the pup.

1. Biting is for your puppy toys and bully sticks only.

2. You cannot bite humans, furniture, or rugs.

3. Pee and poop outside only.

4. Do not eat sticks, rocks, or leaves.

5. Come to the door when you need to go potty.

6. Do not dig.

Some of these rules Doki showed me he could do, and some of these instructions left him wondering if he could do the requested behaviors. Particularly the digging. He wanted to work out an agreement instead.

Animal communication is a two-way affair. Some people mistake it for thinking that if our communication is good, the dog will do what we ask; in this case, stop digging. Doki said no to that request, and his people didn't know what to do with that response.

Why do you hate it when I dig? It gives me so much joy. I don't ask for that much, he said.

Humari considered my request to find a place or a situation where digging would be okay and restrict him to that. A pile of sand or dirt was all that was needed for this pup to experience the exuberance of the dig!

By the time the session ended, I could see and hear the truckload of sand shortly en route to their house. I felt happy and excited for Doki and pleased his people were willing to accommodate him.

Point of View Exercise

Lie on the floor propped up on your elbows, about the same height as a small dog or a cat. Ask 3 or 4 humans to walk around you rapidly. Have the people walk relatively close to you. Sense their vision/eyes being several feet above their feet and how they sometimes pay no attention to what their feet are doing. Feel the vulnerability of the little dog in a room full of people moving around. Notice how you can be accidentally kicked or stepped on by someone in a hurry.

For a larger dog, raise your posture to the eye level of the dog you are wondering about to experience a dog's perspective at that height.

HORSES

19

Little Man

Little Man was a miniature horse friend of mine who lived in Los Berros Canyon in California. He had a vast territory over hilly terrain, and many people in the canyon called him a friend.

The little horse was likely to show up whenever there was a party or a barbeque. Little Man often searched for food in those days, so he followed his nose to festivities across the canyon.

Rumor had it that when Little Man was in his early twenties, a man in the canyon was given the horse as payment for a gambling debt. The man was allegedly a drug addict, and his negligence sent Little Man to wander the hills in search of food. L.M. communed with lots of canyon dwellers who fed him as he wandered.

By the time my friend Judy introduced me to the pony, L.M. was 30 years old, and she had built him a stall and paddock alongside Los Berros Road. When canyon-dwellers found him in the middle of the road one time too many, Judy took action to secure him in place. He loved his new digs, as well as the social interaction. Plenty of folks greeted the old pony as they went to town or returned from work on the dirt road. Many stopped with carrots or to brush him and care for him. He was blind in both eyes and had injured one of them bumping into the fence.

For some years, Little Man was cared for by a young family. One year, the small family moved out of the canyon and into the city, and taking the pony with them was impossible. Judy stepped up to feed him every day, picking his feet, mucking his stall, and grooming his body. She was wide open to animal communication after I had helped her with a dog who had no I.D. that she'd picked up on the road a year earlier.

"This dog had fun riding with you in your truck, but he wasn't lost. Take him back where you found him, and you'll see," I told her. Judy took him back and met his person, who was coming outside.

"Oh yeah," she said, "Jake wanders all over the place." From then on, Judy was a believer.

When things got complicated in my world, I retreated to visit Little Man in the canyon. I helped a little and was thrilled to have a pony friend with whom I could practice communication. He was also a soothing companion. I could brush him and lose myself and my trouble in focusing on caring for him. He offered me such solace. He was a master at just being together.

Temperatures Drop

Autumn finally turned to winter one year, and it was getting cold in the canyon at sea level. Lows at night dipped into the 20s, and Judy worried about Little Man's old bones suffering in the chill. She wanted me to ask him about it.

"Would he like a blanket to keep him warm at night?" she inquired.

"He says that would be just fine," I told her, and she ordered a small, bright blue, all-weather coat for him.

It was a fun day when we met in his paddock to try on the electric blue coat. When I cinched it into place, he stepped aside and began making circles around a post that held up the stall roof. The feeling he sent was playful, and I asked him to show me what he was trying to say in telepathic pictures.

Once when I had a colorful blanket on my back, I rode children around in a circle, he said. I got the image of a fairground and laughing children, with Little Man going round and round and round, day after day.

When I asked people in the canyon who had known him for a long time, they confirmed that he had been a pony at a fair, riding children around just as he had shown me. Now, at 30 years old, he was retired and being cared for by Judy, along with a village of canyon folks that loved him, but he remembered the job with fondness.

Personal Bodyguards

In his service, L.M. enjoyed a pair of guinea hen friends who rarely left his side during the day and squawked nervously if they thought he was in danger or just to let you know not to mess with him. They always went on walks when we took Little Man for a stroll. Even when they knew we meant no harm, they let us know they were looking out for him with loud squawking that mellowed out as we continued our walk.

In the summer of 2012, Little Man's people made the difficult decision to help him pass on. He had lost his footing, blindness had him running into things, and his belly was quite distended. His people let canyon dwellers and others who loved Little Man know when the veterinarian would be coming out so we could all say our goodbyes to the mini horse.

A few minutes before the vet arrived, Miss Judy put on his halter to guide him to his final resting place across the street. Little Man began walking all around the area as if he had more energy than he had expressed for quite a while, which alarmed Judy. She worried aloud that maybe L.M. wasn't ready to go. But like all animals, he knew exactly what was happening, building the energy up for the soul's release from the body.

"Should I stop him and calm him?" Judy asked me.

"No, please let him walk it out," I told her, and she let him lead her until he was tired. Then he stopped to be petted and honored. Vicki braided his blond mane, Judy tucked flowers in his hair, and others adorned him with meaningful baubles they brought.

"What does he say?" she asked.

This is an extravagant party, and I'm the guest of honor, he told me. *It's a lovely send-off.*

I made sure he understood why his people were helping him pass on. He knew their intention was to save him from suffering.

They have a serene place picked out for me, under the shade of a tree, he told me, and it was so. Canyon people placed pictures, prayers, and poems along the wooden wall where his final resting place would be. A lovely photo of L.M., framed and nailed to the fence, was his headstone.

The lethal injection was swift, and a group of men who loved the little horse tenderly lowered him into the grave. Laid to rest in the canyon's Peace Park, Little Man was about 32 years old.

I will always be grateful to him, my first miniature horse friend. May you rest in the shade of your community's Peace Park, Little Man, where an entire neighborhood claimed you as their own.

20

Tractor Monster:

Peanut Faces Down His Fears

Tractors plowing in a nearby field kicked up dust, made the ground shake, and could pin a horse in a corner and chew him up if given a chance, according to a gelded bay horse about three years old named Peanut. Fencing around the land made that frightening entrapment possible, he told me. He was in a panic.

The scary tractors! Gotta get out, was the message and the emotion he sent me.

Talia, a new client, called me because Peanut was training in an outside round pen and spooking badly when the tractors came out into the fields to mow or do other kinds of tilling work. Workers came out at the same time each day.

I arrived on the expansive property, then was ushered to the barn area, an ample open space serving as the primary location where horses were groomed, shod, brushed, and given health check-ups. Peanut was a little nervous, so I reassured him that this visit to the crossties was simply for healing and conversation. He was open to the process, but only a little at first, reserving complete trust in the situation until he made his own assessment of what was happening.

Soon, he relaxed under my healing hand as I stroked him from end to end. After the spine, I caressed each leg with my hands and, in long strokes, released tension until I reached the hoof, where I tapped on it with my fingernails. The tapping grounds the horse.

Before going into the round pen, I showed him the tractor, felt my heart flutter with fear, and opened the conversation about what the metal monstrosity was intended to accomplish in the adjacent fields.

Animals don't usually volunteer a lot of information unless asked, so an animal communicator's task is to be very specific with questions.

"What does it feel like to you when the tractors come out?" I asked him.

The noise, dust, and disturbance of the ground put me in a panic. I can feel the vibration under my feet like an earthquake, he relayed.

This young horse was brilliant and responsive. Peanut said

our consultation, with the information about the tractors, was beneficial. And that if his person could point out the tractors in the field as they started their work, it would settle him down.

I left out no detail in talking to this horse, pointing to the tractors, the men, and their work as we both looked on. My communication included how long the project was expected to take and how we would like him to act when the tractors started their daily work routine.

His person was a lovely and caring young lady who also took the opportunity to ask me questions about a new trainer and how Peanut felt about her. Peanut offered a few tips about what was needed to achieve the behavior his trainer wanted through a more cooperative relationship versus one of dominance and surrender.

It was a very productive consultation, and Peanut's fears were resolved in one visit. In subsequent days, Peanut's person reminded him of our conversation when they approached the round pen and the tractors were working. The horse stopped spooking at the tractors, became calm in the round pen, and all were well served by the communication.

Think!

Animal communicators often ask our animal friends to stop and think for a minute before reacting instinctually. You can help calm a nervous animal or share something you enjoy by sitting quietly and pointing things out to them.

"Look at that lovely tree/flower/hill," you can say out loud or send telepathically. Your friend will come around to understand why you enjoy the things you like. They relay things like: Oh, I see why you like that painting. Vibrant colors!

It's also very soothing for animals when we stop, reflect, communicate, and point things out. I've recommended this approach to many folks who want to take a frightened dog to a dog park. Sitting away from the enclosure for a minute and pointing out what the enclosure full of dogs is about can be very helpful. The dog can feel the whole scene before going inside the gate.

Communicators like me recommend enriching activities like reading and sharing art with your animal friends. Animals report they learn to enjoy some of the things their humans like. Literature, movies, scenery, and nature are all things you can point out to your animals. Their consciousness is very expansive, and it will grow with yours.

FISH

21

Mr. Fish Has His Say

I thought I heard an insistent voice, but I wasn't sure. Animals and spirits rarely call out to me out of the blue before I have a chance to open the channel to them. But Mr. Fish wanted to have his say about cleaning his habitat, and when I asked him if he was requesting an audience with me, he was ready.

An elegant royal blue betta, Mr. Fish lived in a small habitat in the apartment of Jerry and Ashley in the central California town of Bakersfield. I admired his stunning color, flowing, feathery fins, and ultra-sensitive nature.

He was eager to let me know his thoughts, and my attention heightened since it was rare to have an animal make the first communication move. His forthright nature made communicating with him easier.

Ashley purchased Mr. Fish as a pet for her young stepdaughter, who often visited. The couple used the fish to teach Jayla about his species and the responsibility of caring for an animal companion.

The betta fish, genus Siamese fighting fish, is a tropical freshwater fish popular as a pet. They're on display at the front of many chain pet stores because they're both affordable and beautiful for even the most frugal of households.

Constant changes in the betta's natural environment resulted in the development of this little fish's ability to take in oxygen both from water and air. That evolution allows the species to live in water that contains very little oxygen. Native to areas like Cambodia and Thailand, the wild betta inhabits rice paddies and canals. But Mr. Fish was a Californian, straight outta Petco.

"He's a wild thing," Ashley told me, which is what had started the whole discussion.

"I'd like to clean out Mr. Fish's bowl," I had requested earlier, and she was all too happy to say yes. Ashley was reluctant to empty his habitat of water and replace it because she said he would thrash around acting crazy if made to vacate his bowl while they cleaned it. She said he would even bite!

"He's impossible to catch, and that's why I just clean out two-thirds of the bowl and leave him in there," she told me, but she was willing to let me give it a try.

"I'll have a chat with him," I said.

With telepathic pictures and animal communication techniques, I let Mr. Fish know that I would care for him by cleaning his habitat and filling it with fresh spring water. I told him I understood he needed a lot of space and that his swimming area would be severely restricted to the size of a large glass of water while we cleaned the habitat. I told him I would keep him informed about what was happening with his habitat.

But first, I put my hands on either side of the aquarium and held them there. "This is what the energy of my hands feels like," I told him, "And I will need to put them into your water."

He swam back and forth nervously as the electrical energy from my human hands radiated on either side of the Plexiglas. I understood that he felt restricted when I placed my hands there.

Human hands are scary things, he told me, and I said I understood.

Next, I let him know with mind pictures that I would be lowering a glass down into the water, and I requested that he swim into it. I relayed that I was doing it that way so he would be surrounded by the same water he was already used to.

Ever so slowly and gently, so as not to make waves, I lowered the glass into the little aquarium. Mr. Fish immediately swam in. I smoothly pulled the glass of water with Mr. Fish in it out of his aquarium, setting it on the counter.

"I will position you where you can see the entire cleaning

operation," I told him.

Ashley and I scrubbed and soaped all the items in the tank as well as the aquarium itself, being careful to rinse it several times before filling it with fresh, room-temperature spring water.

"I'll be adding a few things to your habitat," I said, sending him images of new aquatic plants I had purchased that would supply oxygen and keep the tank clean. He reserved judgment on the changes, waiting to experience them before sending any information back to me about his preferences.

Once the bowl was clean, I let Mr. Fish know we were moving on to the next step: releasing him back into the cleaned fishbowl. I submerged the entire glass of water containing Mr. Fish into the habitat and asked him to swim out. He navigated the water glass' edge with trepidation and swam anxiously from the glass to his cleaned fishbowl. Movement from one kind of water to another required the utmost trust, he relayed to me, as diving into new water that wasn't prepared correctly could kill him. His trauma was palpable and observable, but he managed to do it quickly and soon began exploring the changes in his home.

I had been watching Mr. Fish for a few days, and I noticed that he recoiled when he encountered a plastic plant in his habitat. He said it was like a sticker bush to him. So, I replaced the plastic plant with a natural aquatic plant and three Marimo™ algae balls. A wild betta tank cleaner, these moss balls absorb the nutrients other algae need to live, preventing algae from growing. As filters, they suck up small amounts of debris, phosphates, and ammonia. Bettas like to move stuff around, so the algae balls also provide entertainment. A natural toy for the fish!

The aquatic plant gave Mr. Fish a place to hide and retreat and a softer surface to slide by as he swam around in the aquarium.

I love these water plants. They feel silky, he shared.

There was one final touch still to be put into the bowl: his mirror ball. The tiny three-quarter-inch mirror, suspended by an empty plastic ball, floated in mid-tank as the mirror revolved. Mr. Fish was in the clean tank when I proudly lowered it into his habitat, but my happiness morphed into concern when I saw his reaction.

Mr. Fish was agitated. He swam around and on top of it, jumping over it into the air and coming down on the other side, then swimming away quickly and nervously.

That's for you, not for me, he blurted out.

I opened the conversation up to him again, surprised at the intensity of the feeling he was sending.

"We like to see your fins flare out, so we put mirrors into your habitat to put you in fight mode," I explained.

Yes, he said, *and it keeps me in a high state of anxiety. So that mirror is not for me; it's only for your entertainment. It keeps me on edge*, he said, nervously swimming away from the mirror. As soon as I pulled the mirror out of the water, he visibly relaxed.

"But it's just a mirror," I told him. "What if you were to relate to it not as another fish but as a mirror?" I asked and began to lower it back into the aquarium. He became agitated again, so I withdrew the mirror.

How about if I live more serenely without it, seemed to be his message.

Over the next day or two, I checked back in on him. The new live, natural plants were a hit. And the moss balls brought him joy. He thanked me for the changes in his modest habitat and seemed happier and more serene than before. With gratitude, I left him to enjoy his new digs and thanked him for what he had taught me and his clear communication.

FROGS

22

Frogs I've Known

It's always an exciting day for me when I have a species on my work calendar I haven't met before, and the day Tracy introduced me to her African dwarf frogs Buffie and Bandit was that kind of day. Before the session began, I turned to the internet to learn a bit more about this aquatic amphibian.

As I surfed the internet, a study popped up on my screen. It was called Mortality and Morbidity in African Clawed Frogs (Xenopus laevis) Associated with Construction Noise and Vibrations.
(https://www.ncbi.nlm.nih.gov/pmc/articles/PMC3314530)

I didn't know why my Higher Sources sent me to read this article, but it became more apparent once I connected with Tracy's frog family. She told me she was worried about her female frog's health, so I asked if there was construction going on near her home.

"Yes," she said, "the jackhammers just stopped yesterday."

The study's abstract stated, "The water in the tank developed visible ripples as a result of the vibrations transmitted through the floor during jackhammering in an adjacent room that was approximately 10 ft away. All frogs in the tanks displayed buoyancy problems, excessive air gulping, and skin sloughing; ultimately, seven frogs died."

Tracy and I made immediate plans to move the frogs out of harm's way.

As we considered options, Tracy said her office was a possible respite, so I asked Bandit, who told me it was very Zen there.

At the time, I had no idea what her business was, but Tracy laughed and confirmed that it was very peaceful in her office.

Buffie was at home during the consultation, and Tracy was at work. Buffie told me she was out of balance and couldn't seem to "right" herself, but I didn't ask her if she was leaving her body. So, when Tracy arrived home, she was shocked to find that Buffie had not survived the day. But there had been signs.

Earlier that very morning, Tracy experienced a deep soul connection as she locked gazes with the tiny amphibian. The two peered into each other's eyes for a long moment. And now, as Tracy recalled their soul connection moment that morning late in the day, she sent gratitude to Buffie, her new

140

guardian angel frog. Buffie had tried to get a message that her deep love and affection transcended death.

The little frog I saw in spirit was full of joy, playfulness, and happy memories. Buffie said her life was fulfilled by what we learned from her and passed on to others. She loved being treated like frog royalty and called herself a teaching frog. She told me that many people learned from her, and the learning would continue from our shared experience.

Buffie came through to many of Tracy's clients after she passed too. Her spirit, image, and personality assisted folks in making difficult decisions or moving through grief. Her service and relationship to humanity blossomed and grew even though she was no longer in the frog body.

After Buffie passed, and over many months, I enjoyed chatting with Bandit, her surviving mate. He had a friend, Hoover the goldfish, in a tank a few inches away. And both Hoover and Bandit were gifted with snail friends, Howard and Robin, that they unequivocally enjoyed as tank mates.

Bandit was a very close friend and advisor to Tracy, and their love for one another was deep. They chatted and shared "love talk" at the top of his tank daily. Bandit was Tracy's confidante and emotional support amphibian, and he took his job both seriously and humorously, calling himself her *main man*.

Hoover Shines

When Bandit passed away, goldfish Hoover took on many of his characteristics. He spent time at the top of his tank, making the "love talk" with Tracy, trying to comfort her in her grief. The brilliant goldfish even allowed her to touch his lips as she sometimes fed him peas. Once, she touched his side, but he swam away anxiously as the electricity of the human hand was too intense for him on that area of his body.

Hoover became very animated, interacting with new plants, toys, and animals in his aquarium. He wanted some natural plants and algae balls to push around.

The sizable goldfish loved change and was a curious guy who enjoyed new things. He rammed into most of them with his lips, experienced the natural plants swimming through, under, and above them, and told me he explored his environment with his lips, fins, and body.

Hoover's personality blossomed after both frogs were gone. He and aquatic snail Robin were delighted to inherit a second snail friend, Howard, from Bandit's old aquarium. Hoover bumped both snails with his lips as a welcome. He wanted to feel what they were like, and the snail pair enjoyed playing with each other and the goldfish. They climbed on one another and explored the habitat together. The three loved the natural aquatic plants Tracy added to their tank, and there was a deep sense of contentment as they settled in together.

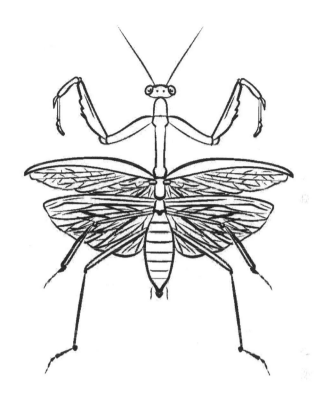

INSECTS

23

Ants March In

It's summertime, and here I am spending time caring for my elderly mother when the ant armies march in just like the 40,000-plus soldiers next door at Camp Pendleton, only less orderly. Mom has been combating the ants for a few months. It's especially alarming because she can't see them anymore. Ants cut paths to their destinations through the hairs on her 90-year-old appendages that rest momentarily on the kitchen counter. So when she feels around on the counter to make coffee in the morning, they crawl onto her arms. And right now, one of her elderly arms is broken.

And the fun doesn't stop there. When mom returns to her recliner to convalesce, hidden ants that made their way onto her clothing drop onto her lap blanket and furniture, and soon crawly things are in her lap. One minute of standing at the sink in her kitchen is all it takes for ants to occupy the living room. Then, on to the kitchen, bed, bedroom, hair, arms, legs, and living room.

Clear communication with the ants is critical. I begin with a warning. I didn't buy the poison, and I'm not in charge of whether it will be used here. But I can let the ants know they have a couple of options in no uncertain terms. I address the queen(s) in this insect group.

"As you can see, there is poison all over this house, designed for you to carry back to your nest and kill your entire colony. Please know what you are participating in if you drink this solution," I say clearly. Several ants are gathered around a drop of poison, touching it with feelers.

Raised by an OCD cleaner, my sisters and I are diligent about keeping counters clean, wiping up drops that attract ants, and taking the garbage out several times a day. After a few weeks here, we seem to have the ants under a semblance of control. At least they're not filling up the freezer. I can't get any clarity on why they would choose such a fate.

Even with all this due diligence, the ants show up in the bathroom sink the next day, seeming to be checking out the toothpaste. *Really?*

One night we call out for pizza, grab a slice, and head to the living room to enjoy it. By the time the piece hits our bellies, the colony has converged on the pizza box. Just split seconds before the pizza is unsalvageable, I grab it up, unzipping it from the melted cheese, gluing it to the corrugated liner in the box, brush off just a few ants, and declare the 10-second ant rule I just made up. Pizza is not cheap.

Aha! My logic tells me ants like pizza crumbs too, and I

declare this corrugated cardboard full of cheese and crumbs an excellent offering to them. That will begin the negotiation as we move forward with our request to ask them to stay outside. I place the pliable pizza box insert on the ground outside, inviting the ants to use their twirling antennae to lead them to this offered feast.

It's an epic fail. The ants avoid the cardboard leftovers as I turn to additional research. What the heck? They loved it in the house on the counter, but now, it's a thumbs down on the cheesy box?

Back inside the house, in the master bathroom, another group of ants is feasting on a dead flying bug. The wing tilts back and forth as they munch. Half a cricket provides the banquet table for a group of thousands in another area.

"I won't disturb you while you clear these bugs out," I tell them. "Thanks for your service."

Ants have been a challenging insect group to communicate with clearly. Still, in saying that, I'm obligated to see if I am harboring any limiting beliefs related to chatting with them. It's certainly possible since the species continues to puzzle me. But if I can't do something or believe it to be difficult, it is and will be. I'm a person who subscribes to beliefs creating your reality, and so it's my job to continue to eliminate those beliefs that clog up my communication channels.

My solution for ant control is communication, respect for the species, peaceful co-existence, and a mutually supportive relationship. I can truthfully report that it works at least as well as spraying poison everywhere, and it's a whole lot more environmentally sound. This approach also gives credence to the fact that, sometimes, we are simply in the path of where they are moving from one place to another, and if we can get through their short season and allow them passage, things return to normal on a day-to-day basis. At least that's how it's been here.

Some days, they swarm. I remove whatever brought them in, and it only takes half an hour for them to disappear back underground. I have the patience to wait for them to return to their nests, and they always do if I've removed the snack.

This time, I offer them a whole chicken nugget outside, and they love it. The ants use the fat, meat, and grease for more than two weeks to keep their colony going. It's a huge success, although it does not keep the ants from coming in if I leave some crumbs on the counter. But each day, as I check my offering outside, it appears to be a colossal victory as a sheet of vibrating black engulfs the greasy mound.

There's a whole section on communicating with insects in my first animal communication book, *Dispatches from the Ark: Pages from a Pet Psychic's Notebook*. Just briefly, communicating with ants requires an audience with their leaders, the queens, and there are usually one or two in a colony like this.

The second requirement is the offering of another place for them to live. In this case, I request that they stay underground, outside, or out of sight. Plenty of space out there where there's also a rotting mound of pine needles across the street that they might find sustaining.

Some days, it's all under control. Other days, they come in and camp out, flirting with a crumb of meatloaf. Still other days, they decide to march through the cupboard, looking for nothing at all, on their way to somewhere else.

Negotiation and continuing education are called for as I do my best to co-exist with the insect kingdom peacefully.

12,000 Species of Ants

As an inter-species communicator, it's incumbent upon me to do my research into any species I want to hear from or talk to, so I determined my ants were little black ants (an actual species!) who come out in the summertime. They like grease, oil, meats, fruits, and vegetables. The worker ants eat other insects, melon, plant resins, and nectars.

Super intelligent and social, ants are tactile, share food and work, and communicate effectively. They let each other know when something tasty is available; when a poison is near; and when any other pungent-smelling obstacle ahead, like lemon peel, presents a threat.

Under her house and in her walls, Mom's personal ant colony is primarily interested in dead insects and meat, at least today. They loved the tiny piece of bacon fat and the chicken nugget offered to them. This kind of ant also loves decaying wood, and the woodpile is a favorite hangout. There's a whole lot of hanging out going on since what you see on your countertop is a maximum of five percent of the ant population back at the nest. Spritz them, and you'll kill a fraction of the population as they scatter.

Then they'll be back, in greater numbers and in stinging mode as a defense. It's better for everyone to find a way to live harmoniously with all life. And as in all relationships, some compromise and consideration is necessary.

MONKEY

24

Exit Stage Left

Our animal friends and companions always serve our highest good; sometimes, that service means leaving. Cats often go on a walkabout, and there's nothing anyone can do to convince them to cut their mission short and get back home. They must do it for their personal growth so that they may be in a relationship with humans. And dogs often visit neighbors and neighborhoods, providing healing and companion services to those who need them. Some animals even re-home themselves to nurture a sick or lonely person or to find a better situation.

In one particular situation, I had been uncomfortable all morning long, and I knew something was coming, but I wasn't sure what or when. I should have known it was a problematic lost animal case coming my way and presenting as a knot in my stomach.

Madison was sobbing frantically when our session began, connecting across the country with photographs of her animal companion, Cappy, on the screen in front of me. She was in Florida, and I did her telepathic reading from my California living room.

"He got out, he got out," she cried. "Oh no! I can't live without him. I don't know what I'll do. You have to help me. Where is he?" and she broke down in tears.

"I'm so sorry," I said, getting her to take a few breaths so I could understand better what was going on.

"He's my service animal," she said, "and I can't get along without him. He's lost. I can't find him. Please bring him back. I'm sorry. I'm sorry," she said breathlessly.

He was Cappy, a 3-year-old capuchin monkey, and he was in the wind. Trained to do all kinds of things for Madison, he turned on lights, got food out of the refrigerator, brought her tools, and kept her company. He was in charge of keeping her alive and alerting her when her blood pressure got too high.

The little monkey was outside in the trees, taking a breather. Cappy was hanging and swinging, enjoying a beautiful day of sunshine out in the trees, and it felt good. But Madison didn't know that. She thought he had run away.

I connected quickly with Cappy and requested that he come back in. He was reluctant, but he did it, and Madison was grateful and tearful. She praised me up and down and claimed I was the best thing since sliced bread, but I was just appreciative the monkey agreed to return so quickly.

Still, I was left to wonder why Cappy was reluctant. He'd said he just needed a break, that things were super intense inside. The energy felt congested, like a smoke-filled room, and I wondered if there was more to the story. A feeling that this wasn't complete washed over me, but I thanked him for going back and for his service.

Cappy didn't tell me much during this first session except that he needed to be outside in nature for a little while to balance himself after a stressful episode. But a month later, when Madison called me to say Cappy was missing again, he told me more.

"He's gone again," she cried. "I don't know what to do. You have to help me," she said with great urgency.

I found Cappy quickly enough. He was back in the trees but not in the same place, and he wasn't giving me any hints about where he'd traveled. He showed me something else instead: why he left.

He showed me that life was a hot mess when Madison didn't take care of herself. There were times when he couldn't revive her and didn't know what to do. When she passed out, he screamed and alerted, but she didn't come around for a while. Cappy alerted and alerted until he was exhausted. But she stayed passed out for hours or even days.

She missed his feedings and became insensitive to caring for him or his emotional needs when she went on a bender with drugs. His most significant emotional need was to ensure Madison was OK, and she made his job impossible.

Madison had friends over for more drug exchanges within a few days of his last disappearance. She took enough oxycontin to become unconscious. Cappy was beside himself. He knew his job was to alert her, essentially to save her life before it ebbed away. He did his job diligently, swinging around the living room, warning her not to do the drugs, and screaming as only a capuchin monkey can.

But she laughed, admonished him to calm down, and ignored his warnings. At some point, he couldn't wake her up. After about 12 hours, she finally woke up, and she called me to do an emergency session because Cappy was missing again.

When I tuned into him, he felt exhilarated and curious. He was swinging in the trees, watching the birds, checking out the neighborhoods, and completely relaxed. He informed me that he wasn't returning and had chosen a new path.

He said he couldn't take the stress anymore and wasn't doing Madison any good. So, he had chosen to re-home himself in the trees, and he was considering hooking up with a young boy who had been watching him. The boy had peanuts!

Cappy said he felt leaving was the best way to impress upon Madison that she needed to make some permanent changes in her life. He wanted nothing but the best for her, and he chose to leave to show that love.

Madison did not want to hear this news, so she found ways

to decide I didn't know what I was talking about. I was no longer the best thing since sliced bread but a demon who wouldn't help her get her beloved service animal back—a cruel woman who refused to help her in her time of need.

I was as diplomatic as possible while experiencing the feeling of relief and exhilaration that Cappy sent me. I wished him well on his journey and thanked him for his service. Then I put Madison on the list of folks I did not think I could help in the future.

REPTILES

25

Python Takes Some "Me" Time

I'm all stretched out against this rough two-by-four inside the wall, Kunda showed me, *and it feels great. I'm spending time alone and enjoying this varied texture against my skin.* The Ball Python sent a cozy feeling, in wild contrast to his frantic person on the phone with me a month after his disappearance.

"I can't believe I was so careless," she said. "I put Kunda's carrier down just for a minute, and when I went back there, he was nowhere to be found."

Suria took shallow breaths, biting her bottom lip. I took a deep breath to release her angst, crossing over into my energy field, clearing the way to get an accurate read on Kunda and his whereabouts. As I sensed the mood of the snake, he was on vacation, experiencing new textures that felt like a good old-fashioned scratch of the back. Heavenly!

Animals use whatever reference point I can understand, so Kunda took my attention straight to the photo Suria had sent to me during the phone session. He was all laid out, half coiled, and half stretched out along a super soft fake furry blanket. He used that feeling as a reference to what he communicated.

The texture I'm on is nothing like the soft one in that photo, he relayed.

Kunda's life had started as a happy surprise to Suria and another snake dancer. A secret love relationship within the circle of snakes had formed, and soon Shiva and Deva offered their humans a surprising clutch of eight perfect eggs. Eventually, eight perfect baby snakes wriggled out of their nutritious shells into domestic aquarium-type life.

"I learned more about incubating and raising baby snakes than I ever thought possible," Suria told me. "I love my babes, but by far, I love Kunda. We have the strongest bond, and it feels like one from before this life," she shared.

It was chilly in early November, causing further concern for Suria, who knew her python needed warmth. Kunda had disappeared, but at least we could take comfort in knowing pythons could go without eating for up to six months. But he'd been gone an entire month by the time she called me, and Suria was panicked about her impending move into a new home in three short weeks.

Losing sleep over the worry that her snake was cold, hungry, lost, and alone, Suria kept the heater going day and night. Her utility bill was through the roof. And to make matters worse, hers was a two-story house with a thousand places in the walls to hide.

Kunda reassured me that he was fine and near a heat source. He said more than once that he understood his people were moving soon and that he would reappear in time to go with them. I crossed both my fingers and my toes that I was getting the message accurately. A lot was riding on it, including my reputation. Still, I felt terrible for Suria, who had contacted two other psychics; we all felt that Kunda was still in the house.

So close, yet so far away.

"I don't know why he would do this to me," she lamented.

Her high anxiety made it hard for her to understand that he needed this time away from all the other snakes to be alone. Later, I discovered he was in a habitat with seven other snakes, which helped the puzzle pieces fall into perfect place, at least for me.

"I don't feel you will be able to find him," I told her as diplomatically as possible, "but I have to believe him when he says he will come out to find *you* in time for the move." It was a leap of faith for all of us as nearly two more weeks clicked by, and the move was scheduled in one week.

One week later, on the exact day the movers parked in the driveway, Kunda magically wriggled into Suria's arms right out of the wall!

"He came down through the portal in the floor of my room that leads down into the laundry. Toward the end of the day, I was standing there talking and looking right at him as he came out. He was waiting for me to be in that exact spot. I reached up, and he leaped into my arms. Nothing short of a miracle," she said, relieved.

I also felt relieved, along with a sense of joy that I'd received the message right. That's when animal communication seems miraculous when it is just another form of communication: telepathic. It's ancient and new at the same time. As animal communication specialists, we are called on to hear the animals' voices when they tell us their exact intentions. It is our job to listen closely and to trust the messages that come through.

26

Karma Chameleon

Mean and cranky. That's how Jillian described her reptilian pet, Karma, and I wasn't quite sure what that meant. But when I asked the chameleon prior to the session, he told me he hissed and bit at times.

Yes, that's right. I'm a grumpy chameleon, Karma said. *I prefer not to be handled at all. But I live in a very active household,* and he showed me lots of action. My human client Jillian confirmed that hers was a super busy family, with three kids all under nine years old.

As my focus locked into the pictures Karma showed me, nervousness ran down my spine. I felt defensive, scared, and on guard. When I asked him to show me why he felt stressed, he said at any given moment, small human hands could invade his habitat, grab him off a branch and whirl him around in the air. He was terrified about it, and it kept him

167

on edge.

I have no territorial integrity, he told me. *I need some quiet and for my people to honor my personal space.*

Karma said he needed a habitat he considered safe. He asked that the parents use this as a teaching moment for the kids. He wanted them to know about respecting his enclosure and the slow speed he needed with the socialization process. (There are some fantastic YouTube videos on socializing a chameleon, but it takes time, exposure, and patience to do it right.)

Karma was most frightened when he was in the air and the hands of a child. He was content to be a domestic chameleon, but he needed slow, gentle handling and a lot of consideration for his species-specific needs.

Each creature and species has unique needs for a contented existence. The seasonal internal clocks of many reptile species make retreat and rejuvenation essential for a balanced existence. At times, they prefer minimal contact.

The Bearded Dragons

My first consultation with a group of bearded dragons was informative, surprising, and delightful. This in-person visit took me to a lovely home in the country where a family lived, consisting of mom, dad, and two young boys, ages seven and nine.

The first identified issue was that the male and female dragons were producing an ever-growing number of offspring. Their human wanted to find out if I could ask them to slow reproduction because finding homes for the little ones was getting more challenging.

Jody met me at the door and guided me to her son's room, where the dragons lived in a spectacular habitat. Filled with bearded dragons of all different ages and sizes, they enjoyed tunnels, heat lamps, rocks, sand, watering holes, and a perfectly constructed habitat.

Beatty, the senior male beardie, spoke first.

I want my people to know that we reproduce a lot because we are so happy and contented. They take great care of us, the children are respectful, and we are very serene in our environment, he said.

The two little boys grinned as I reported their state of contentment to their mom. The beardies sent a feeling that they were in deep contemplation about the matter, but generally a sense that they would see what they could do to slow things down.

Over the next few weeks, Jody reported that first, the beardies stopped sleeping together. Their fertilized egg production stopped, the eggs were less abundant, and the younger, weaker members of their lizard family died. The group had thinned out considerably.

"I guess I got just what I asked for," she said in a phone call later.

"They were very willing to do their part and comply with your request," I told her. "It's inspiring to see how they interpreted our communication and what they did about it. They were quiet in countenance, but willing communicators, and their behavior is the evidence!"

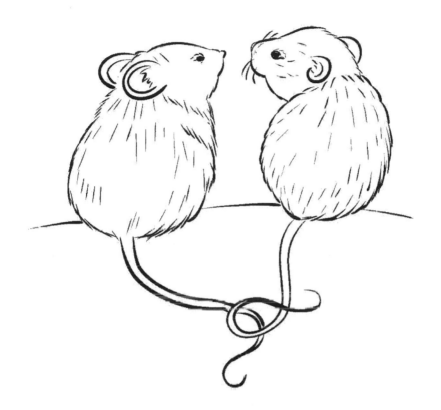

RODENTS

27

Cavy Communiqués

Housing has always been tight and expensive here on the Central Coast of California, and finding an affordable place to rent is a significant feat. Unless you have extravagant resources and a minimum of two incomes, conforming to a landlord's contract and renting a place is the only way to a nest you can call home. The rules set down by the person who owned the mobile home I rented in 2006 included a no-pet policy.

Finding myself in yet another pet-unfriendly situation made me sad, so I turned to Heaven for answers. It was my most common prayer to my guides to "show me the way."

"Please show me the way to my perfect animal companion for this time and circumstance in my life," I petitioned. And then, I went on a trip to northern California to visit family.

One of the family members I visited lived with four other

people and several dogs and cats. There was also another animal there who lived in an aquarium in the kitchen. Spirit called my attention to the glass box he lived in when I heard him coughing and sneezing. My hosts, noting my interest, saw it as an opening.

"This is Wiggy. He's a long-haired guinea pig. Do you want him?" said the woman, scooping him out of the torn-up newspaper bedding and holding him toward me.

Wiggy's long, grey-streaked hair made him look like he had spent time in a cosmetologist's chair with a streaking cap on. His tresses were dyed many shades of grey. This hand-sized rodent was clearly in a heightened state of anxiety as she lifted him. He made distressed wheeking sounds but soon became silent.

As she stood there holding him toward me, I did not reach out to accept his body because I hadn't asked his permission yet, but I did reach out telepathically to soothe his fears. I told him I was not here to harm him, although nothing I communicated calmed him down.

Taking advantage of my interest in the little guinea pig, my hosts sprang into action to show me what he could do. Although it would be more accurate to say they showed me what they did to him. He was there for their entertainment, and I could tell she thought fun games might be a reason I would consent to take him home.

Wiggy let out more distress calls as she brought him into the living room. The Sunday paper was scattered around on the floor. Two large, young pit bull dogs came to attention as the

174

woman carried Wiggy into the room. He became silent and still.

She lowered him to the ground. Wiggy ran for the newspaper that was humped up in a tiny tent-like structure on the living room floor. The evening news blared from the television, adding to a chaotic situation as the dogs came to life, barking at the rodent under the newspaper. He became as quiet as death. He was terrified.

"Watch," said the woman, "He won't move a muscle." The people watched with amusement and glee on their faces.

Humans in the room broke into laughter, pulled the dogs back, and eventually, the dogs relaxed but remained entirely focused on the guinea pig. Wiggy's eyes and body were on high alert. He was frozen in place.

I stayed open and observant. I wanted to understand how these people related to animals because it was far from my own perspective. And if Wiggy went home with me, I would have an advantage, knowing firsthand what traumas needed healing.

Feeling free to share, they told me about another game they played with Wiggy. Because he would try and bite them during this balance game, they put on heavy gardening gloves. Then they hoisted the guinea pig up on a door frame where he had only an inch or two of molding to hold on. They said they liked to "check his balance."

Again, Wiggy stayed motionless, fully aware that a fall from his narrow, 6 ½ foot high ledge would likely kill or hurt him badly.

"I'll check with my housemate and the landlord and let you know tomorrow about whether I can adopt Wiggy," I told them. I had to consult Wiggy too, and I had to sleep on it. I had heard and seen enough, said goodbye, and left.

Voice of Spirit Whispers

By the next day, the housemate and the landlord had given the green light to allow me to adopt the little herbivore. Everyone was on board except for Wiggy.

When I asked him telepathically from across town that night if he'd like to come with me, he said, *No. I love my people!*

But after a moment, he asked me to show him the details of what I was offering.

Where would I be going? What would the new life look like? And how would we travel there? He asked.

I showed him the answers to each of his questions with telepathic pictures. I would purchase a small carrier, fill it with hay, and we would ride 5 or 6 hours in the car to get to our destination. He would have a comfortable habitat, and I would research how best to care for him.

I told him I'd never had an animal friend like him before, and I would need to get myself educated.

By early evening when I checked on him again, he had decided to come along.

The next day I picked him up and placed him on fresh Timothy hay in the carrier. I told him I was happy he was coming along and wanted him to feel what it was like to be loved and respected. I told him that was my goal for him as my animal companion.

"I'm glad you decided to take him," the woman said. "I didn't want to care for him anymore, so I was going to release him into the field out back."

The ride home was uneventful, but Wiggy was the most sensitive animal I'd ever met once he was in his new habitat. He dashed around in his cage and ran from human hands. He squeaked and squealed whenever he was picked up, and it was very frightening for him. I fully understood why.

Nothing good ever happens when the hands get a hold of you, he told me.

"These hands will never hurt," I replied. Often, I just sat, my hands cupped along the two longest sides of Wiggy's small furry body. Practicing mindfulness and a profound sense of being with him or sometimes sending him love and safety caused him to trust my hands, but it took nearly a year.

Even after his trust grew, Wiggy felt safest behind the small vertical bars of his habitat. Eventually, he showed me more reasons why he was so frightened.

Desensitizing him to my hands was my first project. I wanted him to know that touch could be pleasant. The first time I had him in my lap to comfort him, he leaped to the floor, landing on the hardwood 3 or 4 feet away.

I retrieved him quickly and told him, "Oh my goodness, little one. You don't need to fear my hands or me. Only good things will happen when I touch you. I'm so very concerned that you may have hurt yourself. Please feel my care and concern."

Wiggy quietly squeaked back into my lap. I let him know that his fall to the floor could really hurt him, and I asked him to trust me. He was fearful for the first few times and bit at my clothing.

"No bite!" I told him, sending the feeling of my distress at his angst, followed by a message of care and nurturing. It only took handling him with love 3 or 4 times, and he quit biting.

When I met him, Wiggy was allergic to newsprint that filled his aquarium. He sneezed insistently from the inks, had crusty ears, and had a cough from the cigarette smoke that filled the kitchen air where he lived on the floor.

He learned to be loved and cared for in my home.

He was the happiest rodent ever when I introduced him to favorite foods like broccoli, carrots, and dandelion greens. He loved the core of any fruit or vegetable and squeaked, popping up in the air with delight when I served them.

Wiggy lived eight years, six as my companion. He stopped biting and started snuggling into my lap. His health was stellar until the end, and he always inspired me to eat more fresh vegetables with his love for salad.

Spirit's intervention in supplying me with the perfect animal companion under my restrictive living conditions touched my heart. It was a wondrous flow of help and support that I called on more than once to show me the way to my perfect animal companion under restrictive circumstances.

Cavia porcellus is the taxonomic name for guinea pigs, and many folks who have these rodents as pets call them cavies. Cavia is the genus, and porcellus is the species. The plural form of cavy is cavies, taken from the genus Cavia.

28

Church Mouse

Heat touched the pavement, turned into steam, and rose lazily off the asphalt in late summer when Jo pushed the power button on her Toyota hybrid, and not a thing happened. She grumbled under her breath. For a traveling nurse, the breakdown was particularly inconvenient. She called her employer, rearranged her schedule, and had the car towed to her mechanic.

Raising the hood, the man put his finger to his chin, lifted some wiring, and peered under it. Then he delivered surprising news. He'd found an unconventional electrical problem under the hood.

"Several critical wires and cables are chewed through, and the insulation on other wires is denigrated to the point of being non-functional," he told her. "It's the result of a mouse living in your car. I removed the nest and fixed the wiring."

Then he presented her with a bill for just over $300.00.

The car ran fine and without any problems until about five months later. Jo was looking under her car's hood when she noticed the insulation on one of the electrical cables appeared to be shredded. Half an inch beneath the wiring was a cozy little mouse nest!

Jo had thought her mouse problems were over but discovered she was still hosting a rodent that lived in her car. Her suspicions were confirmed when the mouse skittered across the dashboard as Jo was driving one day. Jo then planned to strongly invite the mouse to live elsewhere as soon as possible.

Jo thought of a great place for a new mouse home and soon decided the field next to her church would be an ideal place. This was the church I also attended. As I arrived at services that day, I noticed a car with its hood up and wondered if someone was having mechanical troubles. I considered whether I could be of help.

After services, Jo was guided to me by Lisa, another church member who knew about my work as an animal communicator. The two women asked if I could help with re-homing the mouse.

"Jo has a mouse living in her car," Lisa told me. "Can you help her get him out?"

"I'll see what I can do," I said, as Jo and I walked toward the car with its hood up.

"You can see right here where the insulation has been chewed off of this cable," she said, pointing to a large cable as we stood looking under her hood.

The heavy mesh and the black plastic material surrounding the cable were chewed through. There was a tiny remnant of the mouse nest there, with pieces of black plastic and white cotton still blowing in the breeze.

"It has been living here for quite some time. I thought it was gone, but then I saw it again on the dash of my car as I was driving. After that I found another nest under the hood," she said. She'd pulled the nest out, and it lay on the ground near the car. Twigs, tape, cotton, and plastic all made up the tiny nest she'd dug out of her engine.

The typical lifespan of this small mammal is about two years, so I asked the mouse if she was the same mouse as the one who had lived in the car before. She said no, but that she had been born under the hood of the car and had lived in the other nest before it was destroyed. She showed me a telepathic picture of hiding out during the mechanic's work five months earlier.

With her characteristic pointed snout, small, rounded ears, and a long naked or mostly hairless tail, she was a house mouse (Mus musculus), a small mammal of the order Rodentia. Although a wild animal, the house mouse mainly lives in association with humans.

Jo's snow-white house mouse was actually a car mouse, but she did conform to her genus *mus* with a body length of about three inches. The weight of this small mammal is typically about an ounce and a half. Its voice is usually a high-pitched squeak. House mice thrive under a variety of conditions, including inside a whirring car engine! Most of the time, they are found in and around homes and commercial structures, as well as in open fields and agricultural lands. Jo had picked the perfect location to offer the mouse a new home.

She had no wish to hurt the tiny creature. She rather liked mice but was somewhat distressed that it was living under the hood of her car. Besides the fact that car repairs were expensive, she worried about the safety of the small rodent after discovering pieces of the mouse's nest home under the hood once again. After noticing the ragged insulation on one of the main hoses, she had spotted the small pouch-like structure made of the same materials: cotton pieces, car hose insulation, twigs, and fabric.

Before going into church Jo removed the nest, raised her hood, and invited the mouse to make a new home in a lovely field adjacent to the church. The field was full of underground creatures, including ground squirrels and gophers. She hoped the mouse would accept the invitation, and she asked me to communicate her intentions to the rodent.

I approached the car and sat in the passenger seat. Then I asked Jo to give me a moment to see if Ms. Mouse had a message for her, since oftentimes animals or insects persist in a place until the person most closely associated with it receives a particular message.

I took a deep breath, centered, and opened myself to the mouse. She was quite frazzled at the loss of her nest. She felt out of sorts, disconnected and rootless, showing me a picture of roots that were frayed and chewed up. But she calmed down quickly as I tuned into her.

"I'm very sorry about the destruction of your nest," I said in telepathic pictures and asked her if she was there to deliver a particular message to Jo. She said yes, she was.

"Is it about nesting?" I asked.

Yes, she said. And she referred me to a picture of frayed roots.

"Is that about Jo?" I asked.

Yes, she said. *Jo is at loose ends, so to speak. She has lost her nest. She has made a mobile nest and needs to put down roots wherever she goes. She needs to know that she is her own home. Wherever she is, that is where her home is,* the mouse relayed in images.

"Aren't you concerned for your safety living under the hood of a car?" I asked her.

No, she said, *there is not a lot of smoke or heat in this car, and there are safe places under the hood. There is food in the car and in the car's parts, and this car makes a comforting whirring sound like the sound machine some humans use to sleep,* she relayed. That electric hybrid vehicle whir soothed the mouse.

"Thank you," I said. And I went on to explain the dangers of living under the hood of a car, the problem humans have with mice eating the entrails under the hood, and the offer we would like to make to her instead.

"You could be a church mouse," I said. "It's a high honor. There are lots of materials here in the field and the bushes. You would be welcomed to live here outside, and the people in this place honor all life, so you would also know respect from humans. The offer doesn't extend to the indoor areas, but there are nice areas outside where you could live happily."

She showed me that she was about to give birth, one reason why she was so nervous about the loss of her nest. I let her know again that there were many materials here in this safe place if she chose to accept the offer. She agreed by showing me a picture of her settling in underneath the church.

After double-checking the messages, I ended the session with gratitude. She sent me a feeling of being much calmer, more centered, and grateful to be able to deliver her message. She was happy about the offer of a new, secure place to live.

I also relayed her message to Jo, asking Jo if it would be accurate to say she was feeling rootless these days. She confirmed that it would be correct and that she was practically living in her car.

I suggested to Jo that, as she drove throughout her day, she consider visualizing roots growing from the bottoms of her feet and her sacrum, deep into the earth. Visualizing the earth as her home was one way to stay grounded, even if her car kept moving! She agreed to do that and thanked me for my assistance.

At an evening service a few days later, I tossed a few crumbs into the bushes at the church, and I showed the mouse where the compost pile for the community was located.

Jo never saw the mouse in her car again. The mouse was happy living under the church and found companionship, nesting materials, and security there. I left Divine Guidance in control of the situation and wished the tiny creature a blessed life.

29

Chinchilla: A Real Softy

The softest thing I may ever feel is the body of an animal who prefers not to be touched at all: the chinchilla. I have often wondered how these little furry rodents cope with domestication and the fact that handling them is what we humans want to trade for taking good care of them!

One day, I set off on a mission to the pet store to meet a chinchilla in person. I strode down the well-stocked aisles of dog treats, cat cozies, and hamster habitats with a single focus on finding the chinchillas offered for sale. I had to get my hands on one.

Enlisting the help of a sales clerk, I requested an audience with the chinchilla and the clerk's assistance in making a physical connection.

Unnamed-chinchilla-for-sale was in a nice-sized habitat in front of multiple fish aquariums and half a store away from the other small rodents. The sizable habitat was a round, clear Lucite structure, and in the middle was a half-dome plastic igloo plopped in the middle of loose bedding that made the floor. I noted that this small dome of opaque lilac was cloudy, but you could see shadows through it, so it wasn't dark inside. Paper product bedding lay in crumbled wads around the habitat, serving as chinchilla's flooring and bathroom.

The little beige fellow reminded me of my guinea pig companion Wiggy, darting about to the next hiding place in a quick hurry. Wigs was one of the most sensitive animals I've ever had as a companion. He was a rescue with a traumatic past, and in keeping with his best defense mechanism, he was quick as lightning when nervous.

Rodents like Wiggy and Chinchilla often find solace in the darkness. When you tune into them, you get a sense of relief by looking down a long, dark tunnel-like structure. For Wiggy, I constructed a floorless wooden box about three inches high by 14 inches long, and he loved gazing down the long box. I sensed that the pet store chinchilla had the same urges as I opened the conversation with respect, an apology, and a request.

"Hello," I said, "I'm sorry that you have nowhere to go that's completely dark. I know you can't de-stress completely without that deep darkness." I told him.

I'm very nervous, he said, running to the furthest corner away from the giant human hand descending into his territory. He shivered, waiting. *I wish I had a place to be in the dark. I am never in the dark here. Fluorescent lights above and no darkness at all. Are you going to take me home?*

"No, I'm just going to make your acquaintance. I'm here to talk to you," I told him.

"Be very careful," the clerk warned. "Chinchillas can jump up to 5 feet."

She and I talked about how wild chinchillas live between 9 and 15 thousand feet high in the Andes mountains. I wondered how they felt here at sea level.

Then the clerk casually removed the lilac igloo structure that was supposed to be his refuge, picked him up gently, and passed the cream-of-wheat-colored creature into my cupped hands.

The luxurious feel of his tiny pelt was thrilling. I'd never felt anything so sweet and soft. My telepathic pictures were all about hugging his delicate furry body. The chinchilla did not share this physical fantasy.

"Thank you for allowing me to touch you," I told him telepathically. "I realize you don't like to be touched, so I appreciate it."

His response was an affectionate gesture in my hands, dipping his little head down to hide.

By the time I met the pet store chinchilla, I had admired this palm pet for a long time. In 2020, a pair of them joined my regular clientele list. My client Rose had two chinchilla companions, both females. She had a list of issues to check into and a few requests for behavioral changes. What a great source of information, interview, and delight Silver and Snow became for me. I celebrated when I spoke to them directly for the first time.

Aside from the challenge of living with touchy humans, one of the things that fascinated me about this animal is its evolutionary history and present-day status. Historically raised for their fur, chinchillas that come into our homes to be domestic companions are evolving their human/animal relationships rapidly. Nonetheless, their cellular memories know the unique history of their species with human brutality, and the touch of a hand can recall trauma. Being close enough to humans to be considered companions is an evolutionary leap forward for many domestic rodents.

Before Silver and Snow were my clients, I often wondered about the delicate dance between a human's need to touch and feel and the chinchilla's need *not* to be handled. So, I opened the communication with my new clients by asking them, "How does it feel when humans touch and caress you?"

It can be like being electrocuted, they showed me. *The electrical charge from the human hand can be hard to take. But we can get used to our people.* Silver showed me that the oils from the human hand also created a sticky substance on their coats. It required cleaning once they were released.

When I asked, "show me more of what you experience," he sent pictures of the hands coming down into the habitat and, as they descended, the feeling of a dangerous predator moving in.

Silver and Snow's human companions wanted to know what would make them more comfortable with handling, and they had ready answers.

We need to know when our people plan to 'catch' us, and we need some time to prepare for that, they relayed. The chinchilla pair also gave other instructions to help them cope with what they called 'capture.' For this animal, touching and holding felt like helpless restraint. They wanted to feel safe and secure in human hands without being smothered or lifted into the air. A delicate touch was best for them.

Close to the end of the session, the chinchilla companions wanted to convey to their person that they were happy and that they knew she spent a lot of time and thought on how to give them fulfilling lives. To express those joyful feelings, they showed me the joy of rolling in a fresh dust bath.

"I just love to watch them take dust baths," my client told me.

When I witnessed the dust bath, I could feel the joy deep in the heart of this fur ball with a twitchy tail. I admire their angora-like fur, and their speed and agility demonstrated energy levels I can only aspire to achieve!

SECTION 2:

PROOF IN THE PUDDING

30

Animal Intelligence
& The Science Behind Telepathy

The anthropocentric view says that non-human animals who act most like humans are the most intelligent. A high rating in terms of human behavior would be species like chimpanzees who learn to use sign language or dolphins who signal word or thought comprehension by tapping levers in their tanks. Animals or other life forms that don't communicate in a way close to human language are often considered inferior or primitive. And that can lead to the view that non-human animals who don't exhibit behaviors close to humans are dispensable or unimportant.

This disconnect from all living things leaves humans

fragmented. We see the disastrous results today in the degradation of our environment, causing a disintegration of planetary health and harmony for all species, including human life.

Appreciating animals as they are by affording them respect and dignity means not evaluating them by the standards we impose on humans. Animal intelligence is exhibited in hundreds of ways, but it's different from ours.

A large part of our population is afflicted with the inability to understand or empathize with non-human animals and other life forms. This anthropocentrism, or viewing humanity as the center of the universe, has severe consequences for all life on this planet. It's like a human superiority complex: considering humans superior to all forms of life when in fact, we are greatly dependent on other life forms, including insects, bacteria, fish, fowl, and plants.

Let's define our terms. Intelligence is the ability to learn or understand from experience and the ability to acquire and retain knowledge.

Anyone who has observed an animal can see that they have these abilities. A few examples include the fox who outsmarts a pack of hunting dogs; the dog educated to locate drugs or criminals; the horse who learns complicated maneuvers in dressage training; and the mollusk who tries to escape when he sees the shells of his fellow beings tossed back into the water by fishermen who have removed their flesh. These are three good examples of animal intelligence that would likely be overlooked, partly because it employs telepathic communication instead of verbal communication.

And verbal communication is fraught with hiccups in both sending and receiving messages.

Speaking of smart, let's compare most animal babies with helpless human babies. Most animals have keen survival skills shortly after birth compared to humans, who are protected for many years until they finally learn survival skills.

Science and Telepathy

Science is finally moving slowly toward an expanded explanation of how telepathy works using its own accepted terms and formulas. We are at a place with animal communication in which its effectiveness is undeniable. So, practitioners of empirical scientific experimentation are starting to work on an explanation that can be quantified.

Here's one explanation German Professor Walter Schempp has found. Working on improvements to the MRI (magnetic resonance imaging) machine, Professor Schempp proved the existence of what could be called a light or energy body surrounding every physical object. He discovered that this energy body emits and absorbs particles all the time. These little lights carry information about that physical object at the quantum level.

Tiny quantum emissions of these light particles interact with those of everyone around us all the time. It's our energy body, emitting small light bulbs filled with messages and energy while absorbing particles also filled with information and energy. And because communication with animals is telepathic, coming from the same place that is a feeling, sensing, or knowing transmission, I'm using my energy body to tune directly into our animal friends.

Every cell and molecule of your animal friend carries her history. Just get yourself into her energy field and open to receive the information through sights, sounds, and feelings. By the way, because this kind of communication is not limited by time or space, you can get yourself into the energy field of an animal friend without being in close physical proximity.

NASA's Dr. Edgar Mitchell, a genuine rocket scientist if there ever was one, says science also considers the QH, or light energy body, to be non-local. In scientific terminology, that means "not constrained by time or space." In other words: everywhere, all the time. Dr. Mitchell's point of view on how animal communication works is that the information from the light body is stored in records, and the medium accesses the records.

Then there's Professor Rupert Sheldrake. Educated at Cambridge, Rupert Sheldrake is a renegade British biologist who argues that the scientific establishment should take telepathy and other paranormal phenomena more seriously.

His theory is called morphic resonance. Morphic resonance is the influence of previous activity structures on subsequent similar systems organized by morphic fields. It enables memories to pass across both space and time from the past. The greater the similarity, the greater the influence of morphic resonance. What this means is that all self-organizing systems, such as molecules, crystals, cells, plants, animals, and animal societies, have a collective memory on which each individual draws and to which it contributes.

Sheldrake has written some popular books, including *Dogs That Know When Their Owners Are Coming Home* (1999), *The Sense of Being Stared At* (2003), *Seven Experiments That Could Change the World* (1994), and, most recently, *Science Set Free* (2013). The latest calls on modern science to shed its restrictive materialism and reductionism.

While I'm not an expert in the scientific point of view, I understand it. In preparation for my master's degree, I was forced to come up with a quantifiable study to graduate. This requirement eliminated most of the subjects I was interested in writing a thesis about, and eventually, I landed on a topic that was both acceptable to the academics and as boring to me as watching paint dry.

I do appreciate the point of view of a skeptic, though, since I am one. I question scientific methods that are too restrictive and exclusionary. The empirical way of proving significance is about whether an experiment can be repeated. Repeatability under the same circumstances does not seem to offer much proof! Very limited indeed.

My animal and human clients have taught me that telepathy is real and effective. The changes following a session are all I need to tout the virtues of this healing art of communication that is here today to restore our relationship with the natural world and with our own intuitive talents.

31

Prove It to Me: Anecdotal Evidence

Many experienced animal communicators hold educated views on the application of the scientific method and the request for proof of telepathic communication with animals. In response to an inquiry by a man in Species Link Magazine, a publication for professional inter-species communicators, animal communication professionals were asked to contribute their viewpoints in the Spring 2004 issue.

I contacted these professionals again in 2022, asking if their points of view were still the same and if they would consent to me using their well-thought-out answers. Here they share their opinions on the scientific method, the empirical model, and proof of the great benefit all of us have experienced through our work with humans and animals.

Penelope Smith, Animaltalk.net:

"I view telepathy as an extension of our five senses – a finely tuned communication of energy, thoughts, and feelings experienced through internal and extended sensing. While telepathic communication is invisible, it is able to be perceived if one is attuned to and practiced in that form of communication, even across vast distances. Radio waves are also invisible but able to be perceived with a properly tuned transmitter and receiver.

"For me, the observable positive results of telepathic communication seen in animals and people are the proof of its existence and validity. These results include both physical behavior changes that can be easily seen plus emotional and spiritual healing, which is experienced uniquely by the individuals involved. Outside observers or researchers would not experience the benefits in the same way.

"Scientific studies in remote viewing and other forms of telepathic communication with humans and in other species have been done that show its nature and prove its existence."

Dr. Elizabeth Severino, Ph.D., Animal Communicator & Veterinary Intuitive, www.elizabethseverino.com:

Dr. Severino suggests the book *Power vs. Force* by David R. Hawkins, M.D.

"This work points to the body's inherent knowledge, its pure relationship to Truth and Universal consciousness, and the ability to sense and know that truth. Hawkins is the author of numerous scientific papers and videotapes and co-authored "Orthomolecular Psychiatry" with Nobel Prize Winner Linus Pauling. I further suggest "The Biology of Consciousness" and watch the video, The Biology of Belief, both by Dr. Bruce Lipton. Dr. Lipton is a Stanford University researcher whose work with cell behavior has yielded extraordinary insight into the molecular basis of consciousness, including the conclusion that Neo-Darwinian biology is gravely in error. A major conclusion of Dr. Lipton's work is that the energy of compassion, love, and community actually changes the field into which it is expressed.

"Isn't that what animal communication is? Sensing with our feeling body and introducing great love and compassion into a situation?

"I figured out many years ago what I needed to feel validation for myself and to feel validated by veterinarians and care-persons. I moved forward to acquire that experience and the validation, often putting myself very much on the line. Many of my early experiences with each of the veterinarians I now work with as a veterinary medical intuitive were in emergency situations where life and death were in the balance.

"I was first tested as an intuitive in Vassar College in the 1960s through a study from John Hopkins University. A few unedited capsules from my notes follow.

-K.C. called, dying cat, no external indicators of cause, cat said it inhaled chemical fertilizers sprayed on next door neighbor's lawn, vet took immediate hair sample, sample confirmed chemical poisoning, appropriate remedy given, cat recovered fully.

-D.K. called, dog dying, external indicator of major bite wound, vet felt it was from either a brown spider or a wasp. Vet said antidote for one, if it was the other would kill it, dog said it was a brown spider, immediate antidote for brown spider given, dog recovered fully.

-B.Sp. called, cat dying, hemoglobin level 13, vet said hemoglobin level must rise, prayed for 45 minutes, hemoglobin level then 27, vet said 'medical impossibility', but there it was.

-D.K. called, cat presented with major phlegm and near asphyxiation, okay only on oxygen, cat sent me basement's energy, sensed spores in the basement, subsequent test proved spore presence in respiratory, remedies given, cat recovered fully.

-One of my favorites: A.J. called to say his Dachshund had been paralyzed for six weeks. A.J. said the little dog was not responding to anything and that he had tried everything. He felt there was no hope of recovery, and euthanasia was recommended. The dog said, I'm not ready, but I need help big-time. I took this as God and prayer needed NOW, and I begged A.J. to hold off. He agreed, saying, 'what can we lose?'

"I started praying deeply, and A.J. called during the prayer session to report that dog had fallen into a deep trance. He feared the trance meant precipitation of the dog's death because we agreed I would also pray for the Highest Good.

The dog finally awoke after two hours, got up, walked, and has been walking ever since."

Mary Getten, Marygetten.com:
"There is plenty of proof with many thousands of animals and clients that have been helped by communicators. Most communicators work on the telephone. They do not see the animal and are not interpreting 'body language or animal sounds' as is sometimes suggested.

"I am also not a psychic. I cannot predict the future, diagnose illness, nor compel any animal to change its behavior. My job is to be a link between the person and the animal – to help them understand each other. I am, in effect, a translator. This does not mean that each communicator will translate what that animal has to say in exactly the same way. Human language translators often interpret what they hear a bit differently. The essence is the same, but the way of expressing it may differ.

"Like a language expert, I studied and practiced to learn this skill. Communicating with animals was not a 'gift' I just woke up with one day. I took my first class in 1988 and studied with many teachers for eight years before I felt confident and had enough proof to do this work professionally. The communicators I know and network with have similar stories.

"In my work, I have been able to help thousands of animals and their people. How do I know this? I get phone calls, e-mails, and letters from clients every week, telling me about the changes that occurred after our consultation or that the vet confirmed what I was feeling. I also call my clients about three weeks after a consultation to see how things are going. This gives me valuable feedback or 'proof' that I am communicating well with animals.

"The point of telepathic communication is to relay information. What the person does with that information and how they respond will influence what happens. I make suggestions, negotiate with the animal, and help them understand each other. I do not claim to be able to 'fix' their problems, although very often this is the outcome.

"Our world is full of variables. There is very little that can be proven by the scientific method if you require that the results are the same every time. Math is the one science which seems to be constant – 2 plus 2 always equals 4. There are some laws, such as gravity, that appear to be constant as well, but when you bring living beings into the equation, your definition of scientific proof fails.

"Let's look at our medical system. Some would say that we have proof that chemotherapy kills cancer, yet this is often not the case. The same is true of vaccines and any medical procedures. Sometimes they work and sometimes they don't. Does that mean we should stop using our current medical system until we have proof that it works every time? It does not work a good percentage of the time, yet it is commonly and wholeheartedly accepted. Individuals react and respond differently, and there is no scientific method that can show that the same result will occur again under identical circumstances. There are no identical circumstances when dealing with individuals.

"Scientific researchers can 'prove' whatever they set out to prove. They start with an assumption and then set out to prove it. Almost any hypotheses can be 'proven' according to the scientific method. This proof is based on the law of averages, not that it will happen exactly the same in each incident. This is acceptable science in the 21st century.

"Nothing is 100% in this world we live in – not medicine, not science, not anything that deals with individuals. The animal communicators I know and respect can all furnish written and oral proof from their clients about the effectiveness of their communication. The fact that this information has not been published in a scientific journal is irrelevant."

Barbara Janelle, barbarajanelle.com:

On Double-Blind Studies and the Scientific Approach:

"Relatively few ideas and 'facts' in our world have been subject to double-blind studies. Double-blind studies sound lovely but are full of difficulties. They attempt to look at only a couple of variables when function in our world is very much more complex. Examples of this are studies done in animal psychology and health with mice to monkeys, in which animals were kept in artificial environments and usually in isolation from the larger species. These conditions stress animals and any study results are questionable because the impact of stress on immunity and behavior was and is not fully understood. "There is a large and growing body of evidence that suggests that the researcher's interest and attention can change study outcome. Even something like a lab technician's interest in a particular animal can change that animal's behavior and health.

"We have a very limited understanding about how information spreads. Rupert Sheldrake and others have written about species-level shifts that occur once a threshold population knows something. Work on String Theory suggests that once cells have been in contact, they continue to show similar changes over time even when separated by thousands of miles. This again suggests a wide range of additional variables that we know little about.

"There is a huge amount of material written on the philosophy of science that essentially says that the scientific approach is very limited as a testing procedure and what we learn from it are only approximations in understanding, not hard, unchanging facts.

"Another way of looking at the validity of ideas and information is to examine the effects of using them. Indeed, much of what we think we know through scientific study is based on examining effects. For example, very little is understood about what electricity is, but we have a lot of studies that show us what it does.

"A principle of Hawaiian Huna Philosophy is 'A measure of truth is effectiveness.' We can work with this principle in examining Interspecies Communication. Primary questions are:

a) Does Interspecies Communication change something in the behavior, health, or performance of the animal?

b) Does Interspecies Communication change the relationship between animal and owner?

c) Does Interspecies Communication change anything in the communicator's life?

"This is an avenue that we can explore both formally and informally through questioning clients about the effect of the work. Informally, as I look at the letters I have received from clients in the last 3 months, about 80% of them mention changes in the animal and/or in their relationship with the animal as a result of the communication consultation. Formalized studies using questionnaires can certainly be devised and done. This kind of approach is commonly used in health studies and in the social sciences.

"There are other indicators that Interspecies Communication is real:

a) In almost every communication there is some piece of information that signals to the owner that the communicator is actually receiving information from the animal.

b) In classes, there is always some correlation in information received by the participants.

"These can be examined in formal study ways as well."

On Ethics:

"Another issue raised is about ethics. The Code of Ethics developed by Penelope Smith is a fine statement of the principles that those of us who are listed in the Animal Communicators Directory abide by. Again too, there is the measure of effectiveness in our work that determines whether we stay in business. For many of us, our clients come to us by word of mouth, and if a communicator is not ethical or accurate, the client base will disappear pretty quickly.

"There seems to be an issue for some about communicators earning money from their work. My skill and that of many others in this work has been developed over years of training, practice, sharing of information through writing and teaching, and self-examination. This is demanding work, and we continue to grow in skill and clarity, as well as in our understanding about this cooperative existence. I think that there is no ethical concern about charging for skills used in service to animals and their owners."

Barbara then adds, "The ideas that I express here are a critique of some of the approaches to scientific testing. This is not an attack on science. Indeed, it is part of the ongoing discussion that scientists have on how to make testing procedures more accurate and valid."

Marta Williams, martawilliams.com:

"It is to be expected that many people will be skeptical of the ability to communicate intuitively through the use of mental projections of thoughts, feelings, and pictures. This is something we are taught is impossible. However, within the last few decades there has been significant research proving that such abilities exist.

"There are also many researchers, primarily physicists, who are working to uncover the explanation for how such abilities might be possible, including Alain Aspect (physicist, University of Paris), David Bohm (physicist, University of London), and Karl Pribram (neurophysiologist, Stanford

212

University). The fact that these researchers have been largely ignored does not negate their work. It simply shows that scientists can be resistant to change and challenging new ideas just like anyone else.

"It is not fair, as some skeptics claim, to say that there is no proof of intuitive ability. There is ample proof, and these people have painstakingly provided it. Moreover, their experiments were repeatable and verifiable. One of Rupert Sheldrake's detractors even redid his experiment and got the same statistically significant results.

"Within the field of animal communication specifically, proof comes most often in the form of anecdotal evidence such as information the communicator receives from the animal that can then be verified by the animal's person. Anecdotal data is used all the time in medical research on people, for example in studies of painkillers or other such subjective inquiries where peoples' responses are collected as data.

"I believe that verified anecdotal data from animal communicators is just as valid as statistical data, especially when the communicator works at a distance, neither seeing nor interacting with the animal, and when the data is unique and could not have been logically surmised.

"It is, however, critical to verify and test intuitive data and maintain some objectivity about it. Just because someone feels something does not mean it is true. There should be a 'wait and see attitude' if the data cannot be immediately verified.

"It is the irony and challenge of working intuitively that one must be nonjudgmental and non-analytical in order to receive intuitively. Yet judgment and critical thinking are then required to adequately interpret and utilize the intuitive data received.

"One critique I have of the field is that some practitioners, both human psychics and animal communicators, do not treat unproven intuitive data with enough healthy skepticism. Even the best intuitives I know are not always accurate, so there is always that margin of error to be taken into account.

"However, the overall effectiveness and usefulness of animal communication is being proven every day by its growing popularity with the consumer. People receive enormous assistance from this process. If that were not the case, the field would not be expanding as it is."

Suzan Vaughn, animalwhisperer.net:

Even with close to 40 years of practice in the communication field, it took time for me to embrace the validity of telepathic communication. But 30 years on, Spirit has convinced me with continual validation that this work is helpful, healing, and connected to the Highest Spirit. Fully embracing animal communication as my profession means working as a translator between humans and animals, and in my case, humans and their Heavenly Guides. It humbles me.

Next to decades-long personal first-hand experience, empirical analysis seems puny and unnecessary. It can hardly account for the miracles in my everyday work.

I do somewhat of a disservice to the accuracy of the skill I offer in calling it miraculous, even though in this historical moment, it seems that way. But in fact, it is an ancient way of communicating that is being reborn. Telepathy is, too often, an unrecognized tool all of us use every day.

The uniqueness of each session resists quantification, but it is no less practically helpful to my clients. The existence of telepathy has been quantified by science. But it doesn't matter much to those who serve or are served by these practices. What matters is that it works.

SECTION 3:

IN PRACTICE

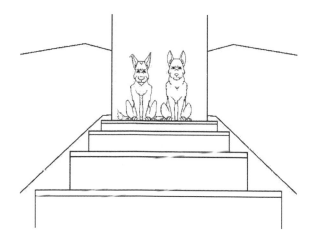

32

Hazardous Duty

Standing in the corner of the entryway, it was frightening, two mammoth dogs with deep, loud threatening barks tearing at my clothing. I'd opened the door at my client's request, who I knew was disabled and had trouble keeping her balance.

"Come in," she'd shouted several times. I was hesitating outside the door because I'd heard at least two large dogs growling inside her house.

"Are you holding your dogs?" I asked her.

"Oh, don't worry, they don't bite," she said. "But are you holding onto them?" I asked again.

This wasn't my first rodeo with folks who see their dog as a sweetheart, while my own experience of the animal is that they are fully ready to rip me and any other stranger to pieces until they got to know us a whole lot better. These dogs were no different. They instinctually protected their frail person, and even though I had told them I was coming, they were trained to decide if I had clearance to enter.

"Yes, I've got them," she reassured me, so I opened the door.

The door opened onto a staircase leading straight to the second floor where she lived. My gaze was drawn upward to the top of the stairs, where both 100-plus pound German Shepherd mix dogs were perched, commanding complete advantage over any adversary. The powerful canines lunged out of her delicate grasp and leaped straight down the stairs where I was already barely inside the door.

With lightning speed, I pivoted into the corner, positioning my back to them, signaling I meant no harm. My client stood at the top of the stairs calling her dogs by name, which they completely ignored. I projected calm as much as I could, and I asked for protection from any animal I'd ever helped.

The 8-year-old, Bruno, barked menacingly at me while the other dog, Dexie, jumped on my back and side, scraping my clothed skin with tough, unclipped toenails while biting holes in my extended shirttail. Clutching my car keys, brochure, business card, and a small notepad, I stayed frozen like a small child sent to the corner to think about what bad deed she'd done.

Eventually, Gina, the dog's person, talked them into setting me free, free to walk up the stairs where the consult would take place in the living room. The dogs turned to her and bounded back up the staircase. I took several deep breaths before ascending the stairs slowly, all the while sending a message of peace and safety.

I didn't sense the dogs wanted to harm me as much as they had never really been given much direction. Their youthful energy spilled from them, and I soon understood they'd had minimal deliberate exercise. They were full of adolescent energy.

We will protect Gina first, they said, *and if it turns out you're all right, we can play!* And that's precisely what happened.

The house was snuggled into a small stand of pine trees that faced a spectacular 180-degree view of the oceanic cliffs of Cambria, California. Careening, colorful twin peacocks with flowing tails were the subject of stained-glass art on the extravagant front doors. But the landscaping had been neglected, and once I was inside the house, it was apparent the dogs had been in charge for months, if not years.

Gina had plenty of money, which gave her one more thing to worry about. She was continually on guard lest someone take advantage of her, yet someone was constantly taking advantage of her. It would have been so effortless, mainly because she was so out of touch. And there was plenty of evidence that Spirit was trying to wake her up to taking charge of her life.

Bad dog behavior was at the top of Gina's agenda, and most of the consultation focused on showing her how to reinforce good behavior. She'd been inadvertently and consistently rewarding unwanted behavior. While there, I modeled reinforcing her dogs when they were calm and sleepy, which was an action Gina had never considered.

These sizable dogs were also restless, so we worked on getting them a vigorous walk at least once daily. I talked to Gina about dog walking services online and in her neighborhood, but while she felt that might be a good solution, she offered several obstacles to making that happen.

I communicated with the dogs about what I thought they needed and what I thought Gina might be able to provide. I showed them the behavior we needed from them and asked for their assistance. They relayed that their primary function was to protect.

"No kidding," I said under my breath.

Gina was mired in the world of indecisiveness and victimhood. Several drugs that treated her disability made it hard for her to make decisions and take responsibility for changing things. As I left her in the rearview, I blessed her on her journey, thanked the dogs for watching over her, lifted the session to Spirit, and headed to my next consultation. I felt like a James Bond martini, although both shaken *and* stirred in my case.

33

The Sweet Simplicity of Animal Communication

Bird-Speak

Boo was a funny bird character who loved his people and his bird mate, Linda. They had been together most of 30 years, and Linda was dying. This long love and association had everyone in the family grieving the loss of Linda when she passed.

Boo's bird-way of expressing his grief, his alliance with his family in processing it, and his avian communication with his people touched my heart. It was so sweet and simple.

"When we cry, he sometimes does an imitation. But he has been mainly quiet, giving himself a big preen as he does after a trip to the vet. That's interspersed with sweet little song calls to us," wrote his human companion.

When I interpreted his message, it meant, *I am grieving with you and showing you that by expressing it the way you do. I'm in empathy with you. We are in this letting-go process together. Now, I am cleansing and preening, making way for this space that Linda's passing has created. And also, there is music in my heart and joy in her reunion with Spirit that I am expressing in song.*

My heart was so touched by Boo's way of comforting his human companions. I just wanted to hug his big, white feathery form to my breast. Not really his idea of a good time though, so he accepted the sentiment while letting me know the telepathic transmission of my affection for him was enough. Lol.

Dog-Joy

As soon as I tuned into Blackie, I immediately heard the song in my head: *I've got the joy, joy, joy, joy down in my heart….*

The picture of this brilliant black lab brought me to why I got into the animal communication business in the first place. Animals are such an inspiration. And this one, Blackie, showed me that his higher purpose was to bring joy.

His person Pam called a week after her beloved Blackie had been euthanized. When I saw his picture in preparation for her session, I was tickled by his joyful energy.

His first message was to show me that at the end of life, he had practically burst out of the restrictive physical body, taking flight into spirit form. He celebrated the release of no longer being restricted by time or space.

Pam was so relieved. She hoped Blackie had met up with a neighbor on the other side who had especially loved the dog. Blackie showed me he was with a light-spirited man who was whistling a tune. A man with a tam o'shanter hat on his head.

Pam confirmed the man she'd been thinking of wore a hat like that, and it was a comfort that these great souls were enjoying each other again

Each animal has a higher purpose. Some bring joy while others bring companionship or comfort.

What Animals Think

Animal communication is often beautifully simple. *The sun feels warm and wonderful on my back,* says the dog. *The morning makes me sing,* says the bird. *I'm finding some great bugs over here,* says the opossum. *I dream of running at full speed,* says the horse. *It's cold in this garage,* says the chinchilla. *I'm confused about what my person wants me to do,* says the cat.

My mentor Penelope Smith recalls one person who followed her, asking, "'What is that cow saying? What is he thinking?' And I was saying, 'Nothing. Nothing. Nothing. The cow is just feeling, enjoying the earth, chewing on the grass, thinking nothing.'"

Animals spend much of their time being, not thinking. And that's why communicators ask specific questions of our animal friends to get answers. Their calm minds are much more still than ours. They are not continually distracted by random thoughts that go here and there. They don't experience a lot of emotion related to the future of what might happen (worry) or the past of what happened long ago. Animals are stellar examples of how to live in the present moment, just enjoying life for the most part. (Naturally, that's different if they are being mistreated.) The main message from our animal friends is, We're here. Enjoy life. So, it's usually not complicated unless we engage them in conversation. But when we do engage them in more extensive communication, they are happy to expound. Like when they share their past experiences with humans or animals, showing what trauma they've experienced, or answering a more complicated question like why the dolphins are being killed in a specific place.

Letting It Go

When they do send me information about difficult events in their past, the beauty is that in expressing their traumas and being heard, they can immediately release a lot of the hurt. They become open to trusting humans again.

Like many people who experience trauma in childhood, my beloved dog Rusti retained some of her fears for the rest of her life. She never overcame her fears of being chased by people, garden hoses, confinement, or food offered by strangers. Even though she was happy and settled once we became companions, I could not talk her out of those traumas. That's partly because, at the time, I knew nothing about direct communication with her. But she learned to relax and enjoy her life of regular good food, car rides, and the love of a caring person.

Our higher purpose as humans is to join in and enjoy the animals' view of simple serenity. Then they can be who they are on earth, and we can learn to be who we are: embodied souls having an earthly experience.

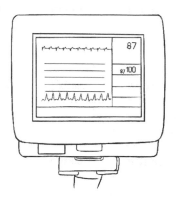

34

Literal Animals:
My Heart Stopped

The loudspeaker in my head was broadcasting *This is a test when my session began* with Larry and Bev, who wanted to know how their beloved dog, Lady, had died. They supplied a photo, told me her name and age, and I took it from there.

I was under the impression that this couple didn't know how their pet died or that the dog had gone missing, and they wanted information to get closure. It was my mistake to assume that because this was, in part, a test. And these two knew their own correct answer, which would mean the communication was either credible or not.

Lady's dog-view of how she had died was much simpler and more literal than the standard human view. She told me, *The blood going to my heart and brain stopped short of getting there, and then I exited the body.*

This message wasn't what this couple was expecting to hear. They expected their beautiful blond cocker spaniel to show me the whole pre-planned scene of the mobile vet arriving, the circle of folks crying, the needle insertion, the light descending, and the heavens opening up.

Like most animals, however, Lady's transition from physical to non-physical was much more seamless. I had not asked Lady to show me the circumstances of her death, so I didn't know she had been euthanized.

I translated these pictures to her humans, asking, "What did she die of?"

"Pancreatic cancer," they told me.

I was confused. With death from pancreatic cancer, I would have expected some pain or a picture of the lower part of the body. The images didn't match what the people told me, so I questioned them further.

"She shows me that the blood flow was interrupted to the heart and brain, and that doesn't seem right for a death from pancreatitis," I reiterated.

"She was euthanized," said Larry, and then everything made sense.

Lady had not had a natural death. A drug stopped her blood flow, and she died.

I did not ask Lady about her physical ailments at the time of her death, only how she died. So, she showed me her accurate assessment of how she passed from the body. She didn't think to name a specific organ that was failing. In her view, the body stopped when the heart and brain stopped.

Most veterinarians use a drug called pentobarbital to euthanize your animal friend. Typically, within five seconds after injection, the animal is unconscious, and within 20 seconds, breathing stops.

The heart and circulation usually stop within a minute, and by that time, the brain, heart, and lungs have also stopped functioning.

In that way, Lady's interpretation of what happened at the time of death was spot on. Her circulatory system stopped functioning. She simply answered my question as she saw it: what happened at the exact time she left her body was that circulation stopped.

Animals are simple, straightforward, literal creatures. They don't generally show me a broad and sweeping scenario of the months of suffering they go through, the vet's diagnosis, or many other details. They answer the questions we ask. And often, we invite *your* questions to ensure we pose ours just right to get the information you seek.

Human communication is much more convoluted. We are emotional beings, and all of our experiences can be a part of the answers we give to a specific question. It's not the same for animals. They're masters at staying in the present moment, so their responses are clean, bald facts, unmolested by emotional attachment and judgment.

I died because my heart and circulation stopped, Lady told me. But because her people expected her to say she had pancreatic cancer, they doubted that my reading was accurate.

It doesn't feel good when clients don't get what they expect to hear. Accuracy is one of my top values, but on reflection, I accurately brought through the animal's message and had to release any feelings of sadness or self-judgment. This release is part of my own personal work, and that's easier on some days than others.

The path of self-knowledge and release is one I would choose again and again on my continuing journey. It's also a requirement to be the best at my work with humans and animals.

35

Mom's Phobia: Fear of Animals

Beware: Graphic Content

Fear of animals is so often misunderstood. I've seen that up close my whole life because my mother has been deathly afraid of every non-human creature since I was born. I include some of the traumatic events in her life here to promote a greater understanding of zoophobia, or fear of animals.

Mom has been in dozens of situations where people did not take her fear seriously because they believed their animal was harmless. Animals are instinctual creatures and often reacted to her fear with their own fear. Her telepathic pictures lunging toward them were images of killing them, or alternately, their killing her. Consequently, her fear brought out the worst in the animals she met, festering a justified lack of trust toward people who reassured her their pets were harmless.

"I'm afraid of animals, and people don't understand that it's irrelevant whether they bite or not. I try and explain to them that it's a phobia. I ask them if they know what phobia means, then I take out my little paper so I can explain. Phobia: an extreme or irrational fear of or aversion to something. But even when I've tried to explain, people mostly just kind of shine me on," says Mom.

The cruel treatment of animals on the farms where she grew up is the source of some of Mom's animal trauma. In some cases, the animals became aggressive.

In other instances, her fear attracted animals who wanted to show her they were trustworthy and kind. In still other incidences, her fear was irrational but no less real to her, and it left her terrified whether she was really in danger or not.

I hope that sharing her stories will help those who can't understand why a person would fear animals. I also want animal lovers to understand that not everyone feels the same way they do. Vulnerable people's fears should be honored until they are ready to work toward their own resolution.

Cow, 1935

When Mom was 5 years old

"We had a milk cow, and she had to be fetched home to the dairy to be milked every evening. Most cows go on their own because they know that's the routine. They go in to be milked. But this cow was obstinate. She always had to be led to the dairy.

"We had a barn equipped for milking cows, and by that, I mean it had a place for them to put their head between a pair of two-by-four boards, and they couldn't get out. There was also a trough for pee and poo where it would run down the drain, and you could wash it down with the hose.

"I was deathly afraid of the cow because she had horns and would try to get me with those horns whenever possible. It wasn't my job to bring her in. It was my oldest sister Evelyn's and Dad's job. Evelyn was afraid of her too. If the flies got on her back, she would switch her strong tail, and believe me, it was a powerful appendage. Now and then, she would hit dad across the face with it.

"One time, the cow tried to kick the bucket over, and Dad wanted to keep it between his knees, but she spilled all the milk. He was in such a rage he picked up a board and hit her right between the horns as hard as he could. He knocked her out cold as a wedge.

"Even though I was afraid of the cow, I hated that he was that mean to her. He didn't even have a smidge of control over his temper.

"Every cow we ever had was mean except one. When she was lying on her side in the grass, I felt comfortable sitting on her back. I was little and weighed about 40 pounds. Mama would say, 'you never know when they're going to turn on you,' so I was always petrified," she said.

Brother James and the Kittens, 1935

"I was 5 years old, and the feral cats at our house in Las Cruces, New Mexico, were getting out of control. Hundreds were roaming the land. Dad told my brother James, who was about 19, to put several of the kittens in a burlap sack and drown them in a barrel of water.

"Instead, James caught the kittens one by one, held them by their back legs, and bashed their little heads on a post out there.

"The neighbor woman there loved animals, and she saw what James was doing. She was horrified and came over to talk to mom and dad. I don't know what happened to James because Dad beat him unmercifully on many occasions, but it was severe because we looked bad to the neighbors. That was one thing mama was always worried about, and his punishment would have been more about looking bad to the neighbors than killing kittens.

"Dad's father beat his boys very badly, and that's why he beat his own son," Mom added. The long history of violence in the family most likely led to further violence against animals.

My German Shepherd, Pal, 1935

"We moved to Berino, New Mexico, and the people across the road needed to get rid of their big German shepherd because they had a new baby. Dad took the dog called Pal. I was afraid of that dog because it was so big and I was tiny.

"Pal started eating the chicken eggs, and there was no stopping him from it. Dad didn't want to keep him chained up all the time, so he wound up having to give Pal away. I was so relieved."

236

Dog, 1938

When Mom was 8 years old

"Dad visited a neighboring farm one day and returned with a little Jack Russell terrier mix dog. Dad had on heavy leather gloves and put the dog in the back seat. He and mom were going someplace, and he told her to pet the friendly little dog in the back seat. She was cautious but obedient to dad's directives, and the dog bit her. Dad laughed uproariously because it bit Mom. Nobody else thought it was funny but him.

"We named the dog Wimpy after the Popeye character, and after we had him for a while, he got over the biting. I don't know how long we had him, but one day he disappeared."

Rooster, 1939

When Mom was 9 years old

"Mom was busy fixing dinner one day, so she gave me this dishpan of garbage to throw in the yard for the chickens to peck on. I took the big dishpan to the back side of the yard and heard a noise behind me. It was the big rooster coming at me at breakneck speed!

"We all knew that rooster was mean. I was terrified, and I didn't know what to do. I knew it was going to hurt me. I used the dishpan for a shield since I'd already thrown out the garbage. The rooster tried to jump up and stab me with his spurs. I couldn't back up because I was afraid I'd fall, and I could hear the clank of his spurs on the other side of the dishpan. I started screaming bloody murder.

"My sister thought the cow had gotten after me and came

237

running to the back door. She stood there laughing, and I was so mad. She didn't think I was in much danger, but I did. The rooster was almost as big as I was. She came out with the broom and made the rooster get away from me.

"There were other mean roosters, too, also in New Mexico. We kept a large stick beside the back door to ward off one who seemed to know anytime you opened the back door. He would come flying toward you with those spurs at the ready."

Pig and Chicks, 1939

"The old sow had piglets, and there were six babies and five working teats. The last one was a runt and not as healthy. So, mom got a box, put old towels in it, and brought the little pig into the house to raise it because the sow tried to kill it. We raised it in the house from the time it was born until it became a huge sow.

"The pig thrived on the milk, and when it got big enough to get out of the box, she put it into the pig pen. The mother was okay with it then. When it got to be big, my sister and I would ride on it.

"Mom looked out the kitchen window one day and saw me riding on that pig, and she freaked out. She said sows are known to turn on people and other pigs. She scared me to death. She said sows could eat you up in just a matter of minutes, and I could just see myself being devoured by that pig, clothes and all, and them never knowing what happened to me," she said.

"We had a lot of chickens at that same place in the middle of the depression. Mom would send me out to get the eggs with my little basket, and I was scared because they'd try and peck me. She'd say, 'Just reach under there quickly and grab the egg,' and I wondered how you sneak under the butt of a chicken and get the egg out. I was so short I couldn't even see in the nest, and the bird was way above my head.

"One little chicken was pecked up and had a bleeding head from the other chickens picking on it. It was near death when she brought it into the house. We put it in a box behind the wood stove in the same place where mama saved the life of the runt pig. We would tap on the floor, and it would come running for a grain of corn or some food.

"One day, a box of tiny furball chicks Mom ordered through the Sears catalog arrived. My aunt and uncle came to visit with an unstable toddler in tow. He kept wanting to see the birdies. He soon fell on three or four chicks and crushed them, and mama almost had a heart attack. It was a significant financial loss.

"Even still, seeing the little dead chicks was yet another animal trauma.

Dog 2, 1949

When Mom was 19 years old

"The next real trauma I remember about a dog was after we moved to Blythe, California. Our friends Winfred and Julie Hall had a dog, and I went to their farm with my sister Evelyn and her husband.

"Winfred greeted us at the car and said, 'You all get out and come in.' I told him there was no way I would get out with that vicious-looking dog standing there. The hair was standing up on the back of the dog. Since I wouldn't get out, Winfred reluctantly said, 'Well, I'll hold the dog, but he won't hurt you.'

"He was holding the dog by the collar, so I opened the car door and stepped out. The dog shook loose of his grip and lunged right at me.

"I had a new heavy coat with king-sized shoulder pads, and I shielded my face with my shoulder, and it bit right through the shoulder pad on that coat. The new jacket was torn, and I was beside myself, shaking inside and out.

"Winfred laughed and said he was sorry, but he was killing himself laughing while I was screaming. Finally, he grabbed the collar on the dog, jerked him back, and hit him a few times.

"At some point, we went into the house. I was still shaking, a nervous wreck, by the time we left their house.

"I didn't see the dog the rest of the time I was there. That was one of several places I never went to again because I was afraid of their animals."

Grandpa Will, 1953

When Mom was 23 years old

"My husband Bill's grandpa Will was a preacher, and he used to read the newspaper on the porch where he sat in his rocking chair. He was an angry man, and every day when the wind came up, and it blew his newspaper, he would swear at the wind.

"One day, he was out there reading the paper just after breakfast, and the dog kept barking and barking. Will entered the house and got one of the biscuits left over from breakfast. He lit a cherry bomb, put it into the biscuit, and gave it to the dog to eat.

"I was told it was such a powerful explosion that there wasn't much left of the dog. Even though I wasn't there, I had nightmares about it. In my recurring dreams, blood, hair, bones, and bits were all over the place."

Walking with My Boyfriend, 2015

When Mom was 85 years old

"I was over 80 years old, and my boyfriend was over 90 when one day we went for a walk inside our mobile home park. I didn't see the dog in the distance because it was sitting with its human mom on the porch, and they were down low. I didn't see either of them until we were right on them, and the dog got up and headed toward the street to check us out.

"I panicked and said, 'Oh my god, Walter, it's a dog coming right at me.'

"The woman on the porch just let the dog run right toward us. It was free to run around. Walter reached out to welcome and pet the dog, thinking I would feel more at ease if I patted the dog. He thought he could see that it wasn't vicious.

"'Don't let that dog near me,' I yelled to him. He changed course and asked the woman to please call her dog, but she didn't move a muscle. He said, 'You can't have the dog on the street without a leash.' The woman still didn't move.

I was screaming and panicked by then, trying to hide behind him and not knowing whether to run or not and frozen with fear. Then he yelled at her to 'come and get your damn dog,' and she finally came and got it. It was a gigantic German shepherd.

"It made her angry that I was afraid of her dog. People often get upset about that. Can you imagine?"

Harry's Cat, 2016

When Mom was 86 years old

"I met a man in the eye doctor's office, and after striking up a pleasant conversation with him, I offered to give him a ride home. I wanted to get to know him better. He said he had just called the place where he lived, and there was no one available to come and get him, and I said I didn't mind taking him since I was going right by his home. His name was Harry, and he invited me to come inside when we got there. I didn't even dream he had an animal because he was in an assisted living facility.

"Harry's cat was in the bedroom with the door closed. He didn't let it out on purpose, but it shot out like a rocket when he opened the door. My heart stopped.

"I told him I was terrified of animals, so he tried to get the cat back in the bedroom, and it scratched him badly. It jumped right in my lap and scared the crap out of me after clawing him up pretty badly. I was moaning and trembling, and he just yanked it up, and it was hooked to my clothes. That scared me to death. He couldn't get a hold of it, and it kept coming back to my lap. Finally, he got it into the back room and closed the door.

"We had lunch together at a restaurant once after that. He called and talked with me one more time, but he didn't invite me over, and I would not have gone. But he told me he had to go to the hospital and get stitches because the cat had severely scratched him.

"I asked him, 'Why are you still keeping the cat?' He said he liked it and didn't want it to injure him, but he wanted to keep it and tame it. And I'm thinking that was our last date. I'm out."

Block Party, 2018

"Several people who lived on our block discussed having a block party that moved around from house to house. Whoever wanted to host a party volunteered. It was a potluck event, so I planned what I would bring and what I would wear to the second gathering of the neighbors. I knew they had a dog. It was a small terrier.

"I mentioned at least twice to the hosts that I was afraid of dogs and cats. And, of course, different ones were saying, 'Well, ours doesn't bite.' So, when they invited me to their house, I asked if they remembered I was afraid of animals. My neighbor Randy said, 'Yes, I remember,' and he promised to put the dog in their bedroom and close the door during the potluck. I said, 'Thank you very much. I appreciate it, and I can see you understand how I feel about it.'

"Well, I arrived, I wasn't even seated in the living room yet when his wife Donna went in the bedroom to do something, the door opened, and the dog came out.

"I said, 'Oh, dear,' and she herded the dog into one of the other rooms that didn't have a door; it was just open space. Then she shooed the dog out on the patio where all the rest of the people were, and I just tried to stay away from it the best I could.

"Once, during the party, I used my purse to shoo the dog away from me when it got too close. I could see Donna didn't like that, and she didn't offer to put the dog away again, so I didn't stay long. I got out of there as soon as possible, leaving my dish behind because the dog was between me and the kitchen.

"The next day, Randy came to my house to bring me the dish. He stayed on the porch and handed me the dish he said I'd forgotten. So, I told him how uncomfortable I had been and that Donna had promised to put the dog up, but she didn't. And that's when he said, 'Next time, I'll see to it that it's put up and not let out.' I thought there won't be a next time, and I never went there again."

There are a few therapeutic ways to help yourself get past a phobia.

Exposure Therapy

According to Psychiatric Times, exposure therapy is any treatment that encourages the systematic confrontation of feared stimuli, which can be external (feared objects, activities, situations) or internal (feared thoughts, physical sensations).

Exposure therapy aims to reduce the person's fearful reaction to the stimulus.

Source: https://www.psychiatrictimes.com/view/exposure-therapy-anxiety-disorders

Cognitive Behavior Therapy

Another method is cognitive behavior therapy (CBT). According to the American Psychological Association, CBT emphasizes helping individuals learn to be their own therapists. Through exercises and homework outside of sessions, patients/clients are helped to develop coping skills, whereby they can learn to change their own thinking, problematic emotions, and behavior.

CBT usually involves:

· Facing one's fears instead of avoiding them.

· Using role-playing to prepare for potentially problematic interactions with others.

· Learning to calm one's mind and relax one's body.

Source:

https://www.apa.org/ptsd-guideline/patients-and-families/cognitive-behavioral

Medication

And finally, medication can help treat phobias, which are a kind of anxiety disorder. Some may include:

· Antidepressants

· Monoamine oxidase inhibitors (MAOIs)

· Benzodiazepines or mild tranquilizers

· Beta-Blockers

Source: https://www.verywellmind.com/medications-for-phobias

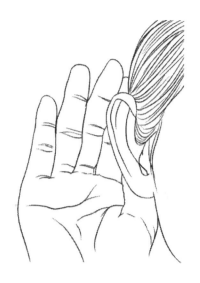

36

So, You Want to Be an
Animal Communicator?

Animal lovers everywhere dream of more direct communication with their animal friends. If you're an animal lover, you may feel called to the profession of Animal Communication Specialist as a result. Like any expert, an animal communicator who is good at what s/he does needs training and practice, sometimes for years.

Experience in diplomatic communications, patience, empathy, understanding, respect for all beings, daily spiritual practice, clarity, and dedication to one's psychological health are all needed to do this work well. A thick skin is also good to have.

As an animal communicator, the practitioner must be diligent but detached from the outcome of any case. Our clients may come to us for advice after they have already decided what they will do regarding an issue. They may be unable to follow through with simple suggestions to improve their animals' lives. They may promise to do something different and then call you the next week to report that nothing you suggested worked. You'll be left feeling puzzled until you figure it out.

For example, a client called me recently and told me her cat Buddy was miserable. He certainly was. Buddy was wasting away because he was stuck in a bedroom, overfed, hiding under the bed, and hating life. He wanted to feel the grass, catch bugs, lie in the sun, and roll in the dirt. Buddy had no vertical space in his room, and he longed to see a point of view from a tree to relieve his stress. But he was strictly an indoor cat, and he'd given up on life.

Negotiations began with his person about how to keep her cat safe while allowing him to go outside. She told me she would take him out if he agreed to use a harness. I tried it out on Buddy telepathically; he felt it would be restrictive and frightening. He asked if she would consider the regular leash and collar.

"I always use a harness on my cats," she told me emphatically.

Buddy explained that, with the harness, he was giving up his most important defense mechanism: the ability to run away and climb up high in case of danger. He was nervous about going out. Images of dreadful things that could happen to a cat outside danced in his human's head and were transmitted to him. Eventually, my client recanted her story about always using a harness on her cats, and she told me she had never actually used one on any of her cats.

Finally, the woman took Buddy outside on a conventional leash. He stayed absolutely still, surveying his surroundings and getting his bearings. She decided this meant Buddy had never wanted to go outside. This was not the case. Buddy was thrilled to be outside. He just needed a little time to assess the danger and readjust his instincts. His person's decision to keep him inside was very disappointing both for Buddy and for me.

A Certain Anonymity

Because we often do our work by phone, our clients may never meet us in person. That makes it easier to treat us callously or to blame us for things that are not our responsibility. Misdirected anger is a phenomenon that's all around us. It is safer to take our anger out on someone we don't know and perhaps will never meet. That's where a thicker skin comes in handy.

And that's particularly true for people whose pets are missing. Someone may have carelessly left a door open, failed to latch the carrier properly, or forgotten to secure the bedroom screen. Even when clients blame themselves, the animal communicator could become the target for those negative emotions. Things said by your client under these stressful conditions must be allowed to roll off. Letting go is a continual practice, as is using a centering meditation prior to beginning a session.

When clients have misdirected anger, they often question your skills, talents, or intentions. Your response needs to be detached compassion. Setting aside challenges in your life, then opening to the wisdom of Spirit, is the only way to get there. That's the path to clarity.

Clients also sometimes decide you don't know what you're talking about if they have already made up their minds.

"I know my cat was stolen," a woman told me, but that was not the information I was receiving. You have to acknowledge what the client thinks, then move on and see how else you might help.

Another client told me, "My horse went crazy when his companion mare died." When I began the session, I told her I saw where the horse had become upset, but I felt it was about something completely different. She decided I had not tuned into the right horse and wanted a refund.

When it comes to lost animals, emotions are on edge, money is on the line, and what the person wants is the exact address of their lost animal friend. That's just something we can't provide. These sessions are highly emotional and often frustrating for our clients.

Becoming a good animal communicator may be a good path for you if you can go to a place of compassion under challenging circumstances. Understanding and empathy are called for when your professional ethics and desire to help are questioned. However, one must self-examine and evolve to be good as a communicator. You must become a balanced person who doesn't take things too personally.

Human Animals

Have you ever said, "I love animals; it's the humans I can do without?" Then becoming an animal communicator may not be the right path for you. While we serve and advocate for animals, we are also skilled listeners and counselors to their people. Navigating an upset person's deep and disturbing emotional waters requires good counsel. They may be grieving, energetically scattered, unable to listen or hear our advice, or unwilling to implement our recommendations.

So far, I've never had a person call me because everything in their world is rosy. The phone rings. It's because there's a problem, and the person on the other end of the phone trusts you to help fix it. They're paying their money for you to get a message to their animal and deliver a message back to them from their friend. It's important to remember that they love their animal friend and want help to get back to harmony in their home.

What's Needed to Be an Animal Communicator

· an open mind

· training/practice

· a keen ear

· good counsel

· compassion

If this work calls you to help enrich the lives of animals and the people who love them, fantastic! Prepare for the blessings and fulfillment that healing brings. It's fulfilling when your practice makes the lives of those who come to you better, happier, and more harmonious.

Animal Communication Classes and Instruction

My preferred way of teaching people about animal communication is not the traditional classroom. How to do it, what it can do, how clients have used it, why they called me, what happened afterward, and how it has worked for them is information I offer through my books, blog, and short movies.

• Books:
https://www.animalwhisperer.net/animal-communication-book/

• Blog: https://www.animalwhisperer.net/blog/

• Movies: Search Animal Whisperer Suzan Vaughn on YouTube or use this link:
https://www.youtube.com/c/PetPsych

"How to Talk to Animals in 7 Simple Steps" is an easy-to-follow video that offers the fundamentals of telepathic communication with animals. Find it at:

https://www.youtube.com /watch?v= ZOK1QTBOdn0.

"How Can You Tell if Animal Communication is Real?" Here are some ways I've been able to tell over my 30 years of communicating with animals:
https://youtu.be/44oiFis144I

Nancy Windheart offers beginning to advanced classes and certificate programs in holistic animal care and intuitive healing arts at nancywindheart.com.

Carol Gurney offers a Comprehensive Animal Communication certification program at:
https://www.gurneyinstitute.com/

Animal Communication Classes on CD with master teacher Penelope Smith are at:
https://www.animaltalk.net/Products/. These CDs are full of information and stories from Penelope's many years as an animal communicator. Some offer how-to instruction.

Maia Kincaid of The Sedona International School for Telepathic Animal & Nature Communication is at http://www. animalcommunicationworld.com. She offers certification in Animal Communication, Veterinary Animal Communication, and Nature Communication.

Teresa Wagner offers classes at:
https://www.animalsinourhearts.com/workshops-events.html. She specializes in grief counseling and other areas of instruction.

Cathy Malkin, at www.animalmuse.com, offers instruction in Animal Communication, Animal Reiki, and Animal-Guided Meditation, as well as private and group mentoring.

Penelope Smith's Animal Communication Directory has

several more people who teach students how to do this work at: https://www.animaltalk.net/AnimalCommunicatorDirectory/

Veterinary Animal Communication, and Nature Communication

Teresa Wagner offers classes at: https://www.animalsinourhearts.com/workshops-events.html. She specializes in grief counseling and other areas of instruction.

Cathy Malkin, at www.animalmuse.com, offers instruction in Animal Communication, Animal Reiki, and Animal-Guided Meditation, as well as private and group mentoring.

Penelope Smith's Animal Communication Directory has several more people who teach students how to do this work at: https://www.animaltalk.net/AnimalCommunicatorDirectory/

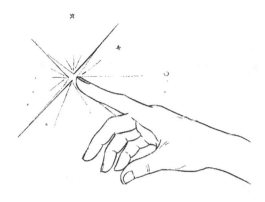

EPILOGUE:

Universal Intelligence

There is a universal intelligent life force that exists within each of us. Depending on your spiritual path, you call it different names: God, Goddess, All That Is, Divine Energy, Holy Spirit. But whatever you call that force, it communicates to each of us, sometimes as a whisper and sometimes as a shout.

When it speaks to you through gut feelings, hunches, visions, sounds, smells, and a deep knowing, we call it intuition. And when we send those things back and forth with others, we call it telepathic communication.

Our intuition is a very practical, down-to-earth tool that is always available to help us deal with problems, decisions, and challenges. It's a natural thing. We're all born with it, but unfortunately, in our culture, it is discounted.

We have come to believe and teach our children that

empirical, scientific knowledge is more valuable than the kind of feeling we cannot measure mathematically, but nothing could be further from the truth.

Have you ever had a hunch or a strong feeling that you ignored? Do you remember the consequences? Have you followed your intuition and acted according to its wisdom? Do you remember what happened? Ignoring your intuition is risky, and most of us have proven that to ourselves at least once.

Trust is one of the first skills in training to become a good animal communicator and psychic counselor. Sometimes the information coming through seems farfetched, illogical, or downright trivial, so trusting is a high calling. Saying something out into the world or directly to a person comes with risk.

Folks expect that I will bring information to them that I would have no way of knowing. We as practitioners are called on to trust our connection to a Higher Source, trust what comes through, trust that we're doing the right thing, trust that our words will be a good translation of the pictures and feelings the animals send, and trust that we can hold a difficult person in the light, knowing they have come to us out of the love they have for their animal friends.

Telepathic Waves

"Communication without apparent physical signals" is one way I've heard telepathic communication defined. I agree that's part of it, but for me, the operative word there is "apparent" because there *are* physical and non-physical signs.

The signs include visions, pictures, sounds, scents, emotions, tastes, and changes in the body. Telepathic communication can make its message known through the smell of something strong, a chill through the body, a burst of tears, or an intense feeling of abandonment, for example.

Messages can be as simple as knowing the phone will ring and who's calling or a sense of dread that a child has been hurt. How many mothers and fathers are you aware of who knew their child was injured or endangered before it was reported? That's the kind of communication that's telepathic.

Telepathic communication is useful anytime there is a desire to talk to someone who cannot speak in a traditional way. That includes Deity, soul-level guides, animals, comatose loved ones, those who have passed out of the body, and all sentient life. I choose only to open my channels to those intending the highest good of all concerned, and so I am protected.

When people learn about intuition, they often ask about the difference between that and psychic ability. For some, the word psychic can be frightening. The word itself is often associated with disturbing experiences or bizarre Hollywood movies. They may have read about strange, flamboyant, inaccurate, or untrustworthy people who claim to be psychic. And there are plenty of people out there like that.

But in my perspective, here is how the two terms are related.

We are all born with the natural ability of intuition. If our family and culture support our intuitive gift, it will become a valuable asset. If not, it may go undeveloped unless we focus on developing it consciously. So we are talking about a spectrum of experiences.

Undeveloped Intuition/ Developed Intuition/ Psychic Ability

Psychic ability is the word I use for those who spend time practicing, studying, learning, clearing, healing, praying, and meditating. And as a reward for hard work, students are offered the gift of the ability to see the future, probable reality from the present moment. This gift comes relatively easily to those who have been encouraged from an early age. But for those of us who have been discouraged and discounted, it takes work and devotion to reclaim these natural skills.

Working with Integrity

Most folks would agree with me that verbal communication is quite imperfect. It's open to misinterpretation, forgetfulness, tone, and a range of problems not only in getting a message across but in later recalling the message that was given.

Telepathic communication translated to the client verbally can also be imperfect. The language is indirect, open to misinterpretation, and requires a whole new language: a set of symbols to be interpreted by the telepath and the client. Every session is a puzzle to be assembled, a mystery to be resolved by the end of the appointment.

Both the client and the telepath are players in putting

together these unique symbols that create a picture of the message coming through. A little dog named Stormy offered an excellent example of that.

Stormy was an excellent little communicator as I sat with him and his people in their Cambria, California living room. The pictures he sent me were crystal clear from where he sat before me on the floor. I closed my eyes to begin and to get a better look at what he was sending me. His human dad Gordon asked, "Why does he like high places?"

"I can see him walking on the back of the couch," I began, "and ending up behind your head. He feels very secure and protected by you there. He says he can also see the entire room and keep an eye on things from there."

Bonnie, Stormy's human mom, said softly, "Look, Suzan." And I opened my eyes to see Stormy seated at the back of Gordon's chair, right behind his head. We laughed.

Gordon also wanted to know why the dog sat in his lap most of the time.

"He's my wife's dog," he said, "and we want him to sit with her most of the time."

I closed my eyes again, and Stormy sent me the feeling of really being able to stretch out on Gordon's lap. It was a very long lap in my vision, and as his little paws hung over the said of the lengthy legs, the little dog's body elongated to its total capacity.

I can really stretch out on dad's lap, he was saying.

When I opened my eyes again, Stormy was demonstrating

that exact pose.

A few days after the session, Bonnie wrote to me via email.

"Suzan, you told Stormy to spend more time on my lap, and he is doing just that! Thank you so much. We can't believe it. He will leave Gordon even when he's having a snack, lie with me for a while, and then go back to Gordon. It's a miracle!"

Communicating with animals telepathically like this has proven to be a great joy and blessing. I had a wonderful time with Stormy demonstrating each behavior he showed me. I thanked him for being so demonstrative.

Helping people better understand what their animals are trying to tell them is fascinating and has made me better appreciate these inspiring beings who are so patient, tolerant, and loving. It also opens the door to gaining the trust of their people, each one a great gift.

Work can't get much better when it enhances the quality of life for people and their beloved pets.

ACKNOWLEDGEMENTS:

Gracious Gratitude

The clients who support me in this work are my heroes. The people who call and make an appointment to talk to their animal friends through me are those who believe. They believe in an old way of communicating that's coming around again. But even I know what a stretch it is to call someone like me on the phone expecting changes in your animal's behavior as a result. My beloved clients believe in the magic! And I'm so glad they do.

My wonderful and faithful assistant Alice deserves special recognition. Clients tell me all the time about her tender heart and sympathetic ear. Alice offers something akin to pre-counseling as she schedules each session with care and concern for me, the animals, and the people booking a session. Thank you, Al, for over a decade of being my gatekeeper and front-line helper in getting my clients on the calendar with all the correct information.

I'm grateful for every one of the world's creatures that share with me what they need, want, fear, and feel. There would be no deepened harmony, no greater understanding, and no created intimacy through direct communication if the animals did not cooperate. As animal communicators, we understand that animals who work with us at this time sign on to a high calling. The animal kingdom is asked to do its best with our communications toward fostering a high-level, mutually beneficial relationship between humans and non-human animals.

My supportive family members get me through the roughest days of doubt and angst that physical life brings. Even those that were not quite sure of my practice 30 years ago but who know me understood that honesty is one of my top values. They know me as a person of integrity who would only offer a service beneficial to my clients. Nowadays, they are more likely to ask me to tell them a story about a recent session because the work is surprising, inspiring, and unpredictable. But even when they were skeptical, they believed in *me*. Thank you, mom, sisters Becky and Darlene, and church family.

I tip my hat to my esteemed colleagues who have also taken up the practice of animal communication. I know just what they go through on any given day, so I see them as people of courage. Being on the edge of innovation is uncomfortable but playing it safe keeps you frozen in place. My esteemed colleagues embrace this gift of greater understanding and direct communication; we are all brave souls speaking the truth of the healing we witness.

Pioneers in the study of telepathy and parapsychology take a hit for all of us when they stand up to rigid rules of empirical science and its point of view of legitimacy. Caroline Watt at the Koestler Parapsychology Unit at the University of Edinburgh, Scotland, is one person examining replication and methodological issues in parapsychology. Rupert Sheldrake, Ph.D., is known for his hypothesis of morphic resonance. He worked in developmental biology at Cambridge University and later researched unexplained human and animal abilities. Sheldrake is a man who has often faced the doubts of his colleagues in the academic setting. There are many more, and I salute them all as they face skepticism in the ivory tower of their everyday work life.

Stephanie Laird, artist-photographer extraordinaire, has helped me with publicity photos for many years. Her talented eye captures the essence of my love for her animals and their love for me. And since she always has plenty of animals, it's the perfect relationship for a variety of photos. You're the best, Steph!

I love teaching about animal communication through short movies, and I couldn't do it without my own Mr. T, Tom Neuman. Tom's generosity in editing my raw footage into a coherent film has helped me reach more people with the message that sentient beings can communicate. He does it all with a willing heart and an intention to heal the animals since this animal lover always has a little dog or two in his home. Thanks, Tom and Barb!

I am forever grateful to my mentor, Penelope Smith, who heard the call to greatness as a sage and grandmother of animal communication and dared to follow that path. Penelope never wavered in her mission, listened intently to her teachers and guides on how best to bring this information out, and trained hundreds of people who are now professional animal communicators. Penelope single-handedly threw open the doors to this new profession after experiencing success with her practice. May she always live in comfort and contentment.

And finally, super gratitude to my loving and supportive companion Pat Henry who shares with me the joy of a lost animal's return home, grieves with me when an animal returns to Spirit, and embraces me when someone comes after me with blame or vitriol. Life is so much sweeter because of your love and support.

Made in the USA
Las Vegas, NV
04 January 2023

64753388R00160